Table of Contents

M000119476

UNDERSTANDING THE INSURANCE INDUSTRY
2016 Edition

Published by A.M. Best

A.M. BEST COMPANY, INC.
Oldwick, NJ
CHAIRMAN & PRESIDENT Arthur Snyder III
EXECUTIVE DIRECTOR Paul C. Tinnirello
EXECUTIVE VICE PRESIDENT Karen B. Heine
SENIOR VICE PRESIDENTS Alessandra L. Czarnecki,
Thomas J. Plummer

A.M. BEST RATING SERVICES, INC.
Oldwick, NJ
CHAIRMAN & PRESIDENT Larry G. Mayewski
EXECUTIVE VICE PRESIDENT Matthew C. Mosher
SENIOR VICE PRESIDENTS Douglas A. Collett, Edward H. Easop,
Stefan W. Holzberger, James F. Snee

ART & PRODUCTION
GROUP VICE PRESIDENT – PUBLICATION &
NEWS SERVICES Lee McDonald
SENIOR MANAGER Susan L. Browne
DESIGN/GRAPHICS Angel M. Negrón

Tell Us What You Think
Is this publication helpful to you?
Did you find the information you were looking for?
What other information do you wish we had included?
Send your thoughts to *news@ambest.com*.

ISBN: 978-1537774626
ISSN 2375-7280

Visit *http://guides.ambest.com* to order additional copies.

For Those Interested in The Insurance Industry

A.M. Best Company publishes *Understanding the Insurance Industry* to provide a clear picture of how the insurance industry operates, generates revenue and provides opportunities for people of varied talents and interests.

It's designed to provide readers with a high-level overview of the insurance industry, particularly how it operates in the United States. It's also designed to be a gentle and broad introduction to the insurance industry for students, new employees, prospects and those who would like to learn more about one of the most interesting and important financial services industries.

We've designed this book in six sections: the property/casualty sector (also known as nonlife insurance), life, health, reinsurance and alternative risk transfer, and the function of A.M. Best in the industry.

Articles were prepared by members of A.M. Best's editorial team. Some content is extracted from *Special Reports* produced by A.M. Best, from articles in *Best's Review* magazine and from original reporting specifically for this edition.

Additional copies of this book are available by ordering online. Details are enclosed in the book. If you have suggestions for future topics or areas of focus, please send your comments to *news@ambest.com.*

Even more information, including monthly analytic broadcasts, topical webinars and other multiplatform resources are available at *www.ambest.com.*

Insurance: Financial Protection From Risks

Insurance protects against the financial risks that are present at all stages of people's lives and businesses. Insurers protect against loss — of a car, a house, even a life — and pay the policyholder or designee a benefit in the event of that loss. Those who suffer the loss present a claim and request payment under the insurance coverage terms, which are outlined in a policy. Insurers typically cannot replace the item lost but can provide financial compensation to address the economic hardship caused by a loss.

All aspects of life include exposure to risk. Individuals and businesses are presented with a choice: Accept the consequences of a possible loss, or seek insurance coverage in the event of a loss, reducing their exposure to risk. Those who don't procure insurance coverage are responsible for the full loss. Those who obtain coverage succeed in "transferring the risk" to another organization, typically an insurance company.

Purchasing insurance is the most common risk transfer mechanism for most people and organizations. The money paid from the insured is known as the premium. In return, the insurer agrees to pay a designated benefit in the event of the agreed-upon loss.

Insurance takes advantage of concepts known as risk pooling and the law of large numbers. Many policyholders pay a relatively small amount in premiums to protect themselves against a possible larger loss. When a sufficient number of insureds make that same choice, the funds available to pay claims increase and the chances of any single person or group exhausting the available funds grow smaller.

In risk pooling, insurers can accept a diverse and large number of risks, so long as many people participate in the insurance process, and they have an unequal likelihood of making a claim. While an insurer may accept risks from a large number of people, only a small portion of those are likely to suffer an insured financial loss during the period of insurance coverage. Risk pooling allows insurers to pay claims to the few from the funds of the many.

What insurers sell is protection against economic loss. These losses are outlined in contracts or documents known as insurance policies. Insurers that cover life and health usually do not cover property or liability, which is the domain of property/casualty insurers.

Life and health insurers cover three general areas:

- Protection against premature death.
- Protection against poor health or unexpected medical costs.
- Protection against outliving one's financial resources.

Nonlife insurers, known as the property/casualty sector in the United States and Canada, in general offer two basic forms of coverage:

- Property insurance provides protection against most risks to tangible property occurring as the result of fire, flood, earthquake, theft or other perils.
- Casualty, or liability, insurance is broader than property and is often coverage of an individual or organization for negligent acts or omissions.

A well-known form of casualty insurance, auto liability coverage protects drivers in the event they are found to be at fault in an accident.

A driver found to be at fault may be responsible for medical expenses, repairs and restitution to other people involved in the incident.

Insurance Density – Annual Per Capita Insurance Premiums (2015)

Source: Swiss Re *sigma* and Axco

How Insurers Make Money

Insurance companies primarily make money in two ways: from investments and by generating an underwriting profit—that is, collecting premium that exceeds insured losses and related expenses.

It all begins with underwriting. Insurers, whether life or nonlife, must assess the risk and gauge the likelihood of claims and the value of those claims.

The companies invest assets that are set aside to pay claims brought by policyholders. The interval between the time the insurer receives the premium and the time a claim against that policy is made is known as the float.

If an insurer has predominantly short-term obligations, asset portfolios should be relatively liquid in nature (i.e., publicly traded bonds, commercial paper and cash).

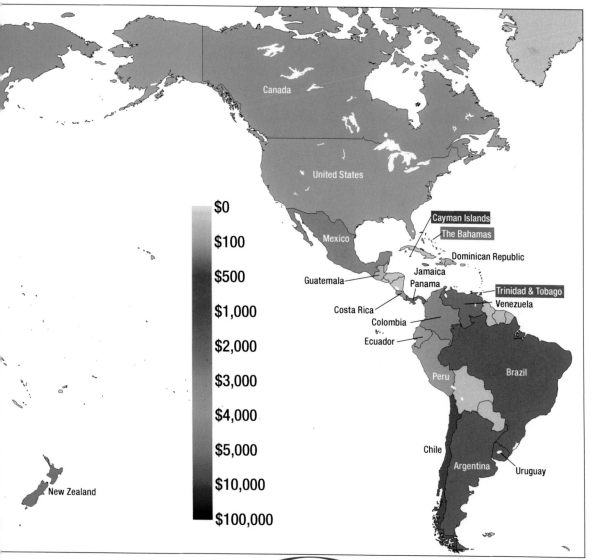

If the needs are long-term, a portfolio containing fixed-income securities, such as bonds and mortgage loans, may also include preferred and common stocks, real estate and a variety of alternative asset classes.

Life insurers also establish separate accounts for nonguaranteed insurance products, such as variable life insurance or annuities, which provide for investment decisions by policyholders.

Property/casualty insurers traditionally have been more conservative with the asset side of their balance sheets, primarily due to the high levels of risk on the liability side. For example, catastrophe losses can wipe out years of accumulated premiums in some lines.

In the end, the insurer builds up a diversified portfolio of financial assets that will eventually be used to pay off any future claims brought by policyholders.

The global recession of the previous decade hurt nearly all aspects of the insurance industry, as many companies experienced declining revenues and investment losses. Those companies that were trading riskier instruments such as credit default swaps suffered most severely.

Few winners emerged; however, the mutual insurance sector managed to remain somewhat unscathed by the downturn. Meanwhile, a continuing low interest rate environment limits the ability of life and other insurers to benefit from fixed investments such as bonds.

The Economics of Insurance

U.S. Insurance Industry Jobs by Sector

Direct Life Insurance Carriers	334,900
Direct Health & Medical Insurance Carriers	547,900
Direct Property & Casualty Insurers	527,600
Direct Title Insurance and Other Direct Insurance Carriers	89,900
Reinsurance Carriers	25,200
Insurance Agencies and Brokerages	776,200
Claims Adjusting	57,000
Third-Party Administration of Insurance Funds	176,800

Source: U.S. Department of Labor, July 2016

More than 2,800 individual property/casualty companies and 1,816 combined life/health insurance companies are included in A.M. Best's files for the United States and Canada. A.M. Best's global database includes statements on more than 10,763 insurance companies worldwide. Insurers pay claims in property, liability, life, health, annuity, reinsurance and other forms of coverage. In the United States alone, the broader insurance industry provides employment to 2.5 million people.

Insurance organizations play a vital role in the U.S. and other economies. They protect individuals and businesses from financial loss. The money they receive as premiums is invested in the economy. Protection from financial loss provides a sense of security to individuals and businesses, which are freer to pursue business and personal opportunities without worrying about financial devastation. Businesses can afford to purchase real estate and equipment, to hire more employees and fund travel and expansion.

Premiums collected from insureds, often known as policyholders, are invested by insurance organizations until they are paid out. Investor Warren Buffett has famously championed the value of "float"—funds held by insurance companies until they must be paid—as an important source of investment capital. However, insurers must be cautious and risk-averse with the majority of their investments, both to satisfy regulators' demands and to be able at any moment to pay claims.

Insurance companies are large holders of bonds, particularly those issued by corporations and similar sources. They invest small portions of their available funds in stocks. Life insurers have traditionally played larger roles in real estate investments, although a portion of those investments has shifted from direct ownership of commercial properties to more liquid investments in real estate investment trusts and the like. Insurers have also funded mortgages for commercial borrowers and developers, who in turn use the money to build commercial centers, shopping centers, apartments, warehouses and houses.

The insurance industry is part of the larger financial services industry, which includes banks, brokerages, mutual funds, credit unions, trust companies, pension funds and similar organizations. Traditional barriers between industries have disappeared in part. Mutual funds can be sold by insurance companies and banks. Equities brokers handle cash management accounts. Banks have become active sellers of life insurance and annuities and other insurance products. Insurers themselves have developed products that include savings, protection and investment elements.

How Insurance Is Sold

Insurance is sold in a variety of channels, including face-to-face by insurance agents and brokers, over the internet, through the mail, by phone, in workplace programs and through associations and affinity groups.

Insurance agents generally represent the insurance company. Insurance brokers usually represent the insured client but can sometimes act as an insurance agent.

The insurance agent (or producer) can be a key component in the underwriting process by taking the role of intermediary.

Top 10 Global Brokers by Total Revenue (2015)
(US$ billions)

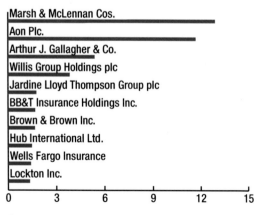

Source: *Best's Review* magazine

Unlike the underwriter, the agent is positioned to meet with the applicant, ask pertinent questions and gauge responses. Information gathered from the interview may become the basis the underwriter uses in decision-making. As a benefit to the consumer, many agents—called independent agents—represent several insurance companies, and may have a better view of each company's risk-selection threshold.

A "captive" or "tied" agent works primarily with a single insurer or a group of insurers, and may receive business leads or some sort of special preference for having that relationship. The insurer often offers benefits, such as health coverage, marketing support and training to the captive agent.

Generally speaking, insurance companies with a captive agent force also may see better policyholder retention. For starters, independent agents are less likely to follow policyholders from one state to another when they move; many independent agents are not licensed in multiple states. Larger insurance organizations may have the resources to track and follow an insured, and they may alert a new agent in the area to where the policyholder has moved.

In addition to agents, the following channels are used to get the business of insurance done:

Brokers: These producers do not necessarily work for an insurance company. Instead, the broker will place policies for clients with the carrier offering the most appropriate rate and coverage terms. The broker is rewarded by the carrier, often at a rate that differs than that paid to the carrier's agents.

Managing General Agents: These individuals or organizations are granted the authority by an insurer to perform a wide array of functions that can include placing business and issuing policies.

Agents are paid commissions based on the value and type of products they sell. Some insurers pay brokers additional compensation based on how the business performs.

Direct Sales: Direct selling of insurance to consumers through mail, internet or telephone solicitations have exploded in recent years. Insurance companies can bypass commissions by removing the agent from the transaction, although marketing and other associated costs can offset the savings.

Increasingly, online relationships are facilitated by traffic aggregators—basically an alternative term for price-comparison sites. The aggregator service links the consumer to the insurer. Aggregator companies receive a commission from product providers when a policy is sold. They also may charge a fee based on any click-through to those providers.

The aggregator service can present challenges on two fronts: The site encourages consumers to select insurance policies based almost exclusively on price, and direct sales are a threat to the independent agent.

Important Functions of Insurance Organizations

Investment: Insurers look to investment managers to make sure they have the funds available to pay claims in a timely manner, match expected losses with investments that mature or become available at appropriate times, and help generate income that will contribute to profits. Investment professionals handling insurance assets have an additional complication: insurers are prohibited by state regulators from investing too heavily in riskier, more volatile instruments. For that reason most insurers are heavily weighted in bonds and similar instruments, and less heavily invested in stocks.

Actuarial: Insurance is based on probability and statistics. Actuaries are skilled in both areas and use their training to help insurers set rates, develop and price policies and coverage, set reserves for anticipated claims and develop new products that provide coverage at a profit. Actuaries must pass extensive exams to earn their formal designations. Actuaries play influential roles in all sectors of insurance, including property/casualty, life, health and reinsurance. The role of actuaries continues to grow as noninsurance industries—such as hedge funds, risk modelers and capital markets participants—become involved in developing risk products and programs.

Underwriting: At the heart of insurance is the art and science of assuming risk. Underwriters use a combination of data gathering and analysis, interviewing and professional knowledge to evaluate whether a given risk meets the insurer's standards for prudent risk evaluation. Their job is to evaluate whether given risks can be covered and, if so, under what terms. Underwriting departments often have the authority to accept or reject risks. Perhaps the most significant responsibility of underwriters is to determine premium that recognizes the likelihood of a claim and enables the insurer to earn a profit. Some of the process has been automated, such as when auto and homeowners insurers access information like driving and property records. Applicants for life insurance and some forms of health coverage may be asked to obtain medical evaluations.

Claims: Sometimes called the actual "product" that insurance companies deliver, claims departments usually operate in two areas: at the offices of the insurer and in the field through claims adjusters. Claims are requests for payment based on losses believed by the policyholder to be covered under an insurance policy. Claims personnel evaluate the request and determine the amount of loss the insurer should pay. Requests for claims payment can come directly to insurers or be handled by agents and brokers working directly with the insured. Claims adjusters can work directly for an insurer or operate as independent businesses that can work for multiple insurers. Claims adjusters often have designated levels of authority to settle claims. Adjusters serve as claims investigators and sometimes conduct elaborate investigations in the event of suspected fraudulent claims.

World's Largest Insurance Companies
Based on 2014 nonbanking assets.
(US$ thousands)

2014	2013	Company Name	Country of Domicile		2014 Nonbanking Assets	% Change*
1	1	AXA S.A.	France		965,363,878	11.31
2	2	Allianz SE	Germany		930,297,464	14.03
3	3	MetLife Inc.	United States		902,337,000	1.92
4	5	Prudential Financial Inc.	United States		766,655,000	4.77
5	4	Japan Post Insurance Co., Ltd.	Japan		709,778,957	-2.50
6	7	Legal & General Group Plc	United Kingdom		620,665,630	9.09
7	6	Assicurazioni Generali S.p.A.	Italy		609,402,161	11.49
8	10	Prudential plc	United Kingdom		573,521,494	13.28
9	14	Berkshire Hathaway Inc.	United States		526,186,000	8.51
10	8	Nippon Life Insurance Company	Japan		523,679,990	9.74
11	13	Aegon N.V.	Netherlands		516,510,871	20.79
12	9	American International Group, Inc.	United States		515,581,000	-4.76
13	15	Manulife Financial Corporation	Canada		498,347,101	12.81
14	12	CNP Assurances	France		480,631,465	8.21
15	11	National Mut Ins Fed Agricultural Coop.	Japan		457,793,558	3.49
16	19	China Life Insurance (Group) Company	China		447,452,906	14.11
17	16	Aviva plc	United Kingdom		443,835,895	1.45
18	20	Dai-ichi Life Insurance Company, Limited	Japan		416,589,172	32.18
19	17	Zurich Insurance Group Ltd.	Switzerland		406,529,000	-2.05
20	18	Credit Agricole Assurances	France		400,269,121	13.00
21	23	Ping An Ins (Group) Co. of China Ltd.	China		367,890,917	12.72
22	21	Munich Reinsurance Company	Germany		331,833,272	7.34
23	...	Life Insurance Corporation of India	India		322,115,868	15.80
24	25	Standard Life Plc	United Kingdom		316,270,687	7.64
25	24	Great-West Lifeco Inc.	Canada		306,805,411	9.46

Based on 2014 net premiums written.
(US$ thousands)

2014	2013	Company Name	Country of Domicile		2014 Net Premiums Written	% Change*
1	2	UnitedHealth Group Incorporated[1]	United States		115,302,000	5.24
2	1	AXA S.A.	France		99,600,186	1.93
3	3	Allianz SE	Germany		84,386,952	2.83
4	4	Assicurazioni Generali S.p.A.	Italy		78,157,002	6.17
5	6	Anthem, Inc.	United States		68,712,400	4.08
6	7	China Life Insurance (Group) Company	China		65,714,675	5.17
7	8	State Farm Group[2]	United States		63,168,857	4.61
8	10	Kaiser Foundation Group of Health Plans[2]	United States		62,658,963	6.69
9	5	Munich Reinsurance Company	Germany		57,406,710	-4.41
10	17	Aetna Inc.[1]	United States		51,748,500	23.69
11	15	People's Ins Co. (Group) of China Ltd.	China		51,538,465	16.06
12	12	Prudential plc	United Kingdom		49,760,062	7.33
13	11	Japan Post Insurance Co., Ltd.	Japan		49,724,774	0.68
14	18	Ping An Ins (Group) Co. of China Ltd.	China		49,157,193	21.67
15	13	Zurich Insurance Group Ltd.	Switzerland		48,680,000	0.78
16	9	National Mut Ins Fed Agricultural Coop.	Japan		48,361,346	-5.38
17	20	Humana Inc.[1]	United States		45,959,000	18.36
18	16	Dai-ichi Life Insurance Company, Limited	Japan		45,412,081	24.80
19	14	Nippon Life Insurance Company	Japan		44,880,842	10.51
20	23	Berkshire Hathaway Inc.	United States		42,433,000	14.04
21	22	MetLife Inc.	United States		39,067,000	3.70
22	19	Life Insurance Corporation of India	India		38,293,295	1.13
23	21	American International Group, Inc.	United States		37,865,000	-0.80
24	24	CNP Assurances	France		36,405,153	14.91
25	...	Liberty Mutual Holding Company Inc.	United States		36,275,000	3.30

* Percent change is based upon local currency.
1 Premiums shown are earned premiums.
2 A.M. Best consolidation; U.S. companies only
Source: BESTLINK

Insurance Entities

Ownership of traditional insurance companies generally comes in two structures, mutual and stock, although insuring entities may take a number of other forms, including reciprocal exchanges and risk retention groups. Mutual insurers are owned by and run for the benefit of their policyholders. Relative to insurance companies with shareholder ownership, mutual insurers have less access to the capital markets to raise money. Many mutual insurance companies have been formed by people or businesses with a common need, such as farmers. Mutuals pay a return of premium or "policyholder dividend" back to the policyholder if the company has strong financial results and a lower-than-expected number of claims. Policyholders also have the ability to vote on company leadership and have a say in certain corporate governance issues.

Reciprocal insurance companies resemble mutual companies. Whereas a mutual insurance company is incorporated, the reciprocal company is run by a management company, referred to as an attorney-in-fact.

Many mutuals were able to grow during the credit crunch of the late 2000s. Their growth is limited, however, because capital has to be generated internally, as there are no shares to sell. Some top (former) mutual insurance companies, including Metropolitan Life and Prudential, have demutualized to become shareholder-owned public companies. Typically, demutualization is done to raise capital or expand operations. Other companies,

Top 10 U.S. Holding Companies, 2015
Ranked by Assets

Rank	Company Name	AMB#	2015 Total Assets ($000)	2014 Total Assets ($000)	% Change
1	MetLife Inc.	058175	877,933,000	902,337,000	-2.7
2	Prudential Financial Inc.	058182	757,388,000	766,655,000	-1.2
3	Berkshire Hathaway Inc.	058334	552,257,000	525,867,000	5.0
4	American International Group, Inc.	058702	496,943,000	515,581,000	-3.6
5	Lincoln National Corporation	058709	251,937,000	253,377,000	-0.6
6	Hartford Financial Services Group Inc.	058707	228,348,000	245,013,000	-6.8
7	Principal Financial Group Inc.	058179	218,685,900	219,087,000	-0.2
8	Voya Financial Inc.	050817	218,249,600	226,930,700	-3.8
9	Ameriprise Financial Inc.	050542	145,342,000	148,810,000	-2.3
10	Pacific Mutual Holding Company	050799	137,279,000	137,048,000	0.2

Ranked by Revenue

Rank	Company Name	AMB#	2015 Total Revenue ($000)	2014 Total Revenue ($000)	% Change
1	Berkshire Hathaway Inc.	058334	210,821,000	194,673,000	8.3
2	UnitedHealth Group Incorporated	058106	157,107,000	130,474,000	20.4
3	Anthem, Inc.	058180	79,165,800	73,874,100	7.2
4	MetLife Inc.	058175	69,951,000	73,316,000	-4.6
5	Aetna Inc.	058700	60,336,500	58,003,200	4.0
6	American International Group, Inc.	058702	58,327,000	66,603,000	-12.4
7	Prudential Financial Inc.	058182	57,119,000	56,083,000	1.8
8	Humana Inc.	058052	54,559,000	48,500,000	12.5
9	Cigna Corporation	058703	37,876,000	34,914,000	8.5
10	Liberty Mutual Holding Company Inc.	051114	37,617,000	37,721,000	-0.3

Source: BESTLINK Holding Companies database

including Pacific Life and Liberty Mutual, took an intermediate step and became part of a mutual holding company structure, which gave them greater access to the capital markets.

A holding company structure, employed primarily in the United States, provides easier access to the capital markets, whereby shares can be sold to help raise capital. The holding company owns a significant amount, if not all, of another company's or other companies' common stock. Many insurance companies are part of a holding company structure, with the publicly traded parent company owning stock of the subsidiary or the controlled insurance company (or companies).

Captive insurance companies are formed to insure the risks of their parent group or groups, and sometimes will insure risks of the group's customers. Captive insurers have become higher-profile in recent years after many U.S. states and some international jurisdictions adopted legislation and rules encouraging captives to locate in their domiciles.

A risk retention group is a liability insurance company owned by its policyholders. Membership is limited to people in the same business or activity, which exposes them to similar liability risks. The purpose is to assume and spread liability exposure to group members and to provide an alternative risk financing mechanism for liability. These entities are formed under the Liability Risk Retention Act of 1986.

Structural differences between stock and mutual insurance companies affect business decisions. Stock companies have to answer to owners and policyholders, so if management's investment strategies are carried out with shareholder expectations in mind — seizing opportunities for growth and profit — they may be acting at the expense of policyholders. Mutuals, on the other hand, are owned by the policyholders, so the focus likely will be on affordability and dividends.

Observers have struggled to make meaningful comparisons of profitability generated by public and mutual companies. One thing is certain, however: no particular organizational structure is a cure-all for poorly conceived or executed strategies.

Spotlight: Under Disruption

Technological advances are forcing the often-predictable insurance industry to embrace innovation as the antidote to potential disruptions to business as usual.

"What we're seeing is hundreds of small startups that see the risk analysis industry and the insurance industry as a mega industry ripe for disruption, because it hasn't seen a huge amount of change yet, and it will," Neil Jacobstein, chair of artificial intelligence and robotics at Singularity University, said.

"The startups are using the web, and they're creating their own risk pools and they're using algorithms instead of people to do the underlying assessment," Jacobstein said. "In some cases they're using a more powerful combination of algorithms and people, and that's a very potent combination. I think we'll see that truly disrupting the insurance industry over the next few years."

Whether it is online insurance comparison tools circumventing the typical agent/broker-customer relationship, or telematics calculating a driver's or homeowner's risk, or weather data used to automatically trigger claims for agriculture risk, potential disruptors to the insurance industry are gathering along the boundaries that used to separate insurance from uncovered economic loss.

"Technology innovation will make some aspects of current insurance obsolete through shifting risk pools," according to the 2015 Accenture Strategy report, *Beyond insurance: Embracing innovation to monetize disruption.*

The report mentions that new competitors such as Google and Walmart have sought to disrupt the traditional insurance business model. "But every business model has a beginning and an end," according to the report. "Most insurers have been investing only in their current business model, but firms that understand the changes at hand are repositioning themselves and pursuing growth options to move beyond insurance."

Stephen O'Hearn, global insurance leader, PwC, identifies three areas where insurers are changing in response to the greater impact of digitalization and real-time analysis.

- **Customer experience.** "Customers are no longer looking for a financial planner to come into their home, to work with young couples to plan their kids' college education or their own retirement. They're doing it online—robo-advice, for example."
- **Data analytics.** "Data is transforming the insurer from being a

Neil Jacobstein

relatively passive payer of losses to a preventative risk adviser. Three-fourths of the consumers are willing to put a sensor in their car or home if it would help them reduce their premiums. That means that the insurer can monitor the functioning of the home, the furnace for example, send in a repair team to repair a broken furnace before a loss is incurred. Think about that. The insurer is preventing a loss instead of just pulling monies paying a claim."

- **Cost innovation.** "Digital enhancements through artificial intelligence and robotics are taking costs out of a cost structure that needs to be reduced."

So is this a revolution or merely evolution?

"The insurance industry has been using artificial intelligence for over three decades," Singularity's Jacobstein said. "It's gotten better and better."

The overall insurance industry stands to gain. "We're moving from opinion-based assessment of the data to evidence-based assessment, and we're using high-dimensionality algorithms to give us inhumanly good actuarial predictions in the

Linda Conrad

automotive industry, in the airline industry, risk industry and also in the health industry," Jacobstein added.

While much of this may be seen as incremental technological progression, the potential remains for larger-scale disruption.

"We're seeing all sorts of looming challenges around the digitalization of the insurance industry, the changes in distribution, changes in manufacturing, supply chain, the emergence of cyberthreats and very disruptive forces that are looming on the outside, big data, enormous challenges for everyone in every aspect of the business," Willis Re President Andrew Newman said. "Innovation is coming. We're seeing new forms of distribution, new forms of technology, peer to peer, new products being revealed by insurers dealing with the cyber crisis or the perception of a cyberthreat."

"It's important to do a lot of evaluation, risk assessment and mitigation around the possible digital disruptions," said Linda Conrad, CEO and Chief Risk Officer at Climassure formerly with Zurich Financial Services. "It's not just looking at the data side of data loss potential but actually trying to say, "If something like a cyber disruption happens, how is it going to take us down from delivering to our shareholders and our customers? What resources could be unavailable? What locations might be down, etc.?"

Zurich was involved with the *World Economic Forum Global Risk Report*, which identified cyberrisk as "the single most impactful risk for business," Conrad said.

Not all disruptors are successful, though. "The low barriers to entry to E&S carriers into our space makes it a real challenge as new markets come in and tend to disrupt a bit and then fade out after a couple of years when they find out it's a little harder than they thought," said Art Davis, president of excess and surplus carrier Argo Group U.S.

Technology that can disrupt traditional insurance business can also help it compete. "Four out of every five insurers will say their biggest challenge is keeping the lights on with their existing business," said Mary Trussell of KPMG International. "This is one of the things that insurers are having to learn, to be much more nimble and agile. This is where technology can really enable that agility."

"If you don't have to change the culture, and you are small, you can move more nimbly," said Brian Duperreault, chairman and CEO of Hamilton Group. "You can go quicker. You can try things. You can experiment. That's what the industry's wrestling with, these large institutions trying to change, and these smaller, new entrants trying to beat them to the punch."

Andrew Boyle, co-owner of Boyle Transportation, has firsthand experience with technology disrupting and ultimately improving business.

Andrew Boyle

For evidence, he points to new regulatory requirements for truckers. "The requirement for trucks to have electronic log-in devices, which tie in to the engine computer and prohibit a truck driver from falsifying logs, will be required by December of 2017," he said. "It likely will lead bad actors to either get out of the industry or become compliant. In the short term there will be some disruption and perhaps a shrinking capacity. However, it will be a long-term net positive for our industry, because it will result in a safe work environment."

"Large established insurers are used to big decisions, big product launches, big system implementations, big M&A," O'Hearn said. "This is about little decisions. This is about experimentation. Some of those experiments work; some don't. You learn from the ones that don't, and you move on and make more decisions. Quick little decisions is a real culture change for the insurance industry.

"One of the biggest challenges for the insurers is to mainstream this innovation. Getting that inculcated into the mainstream of a large company, that's a challenge," O'Hearn added. "They're working their way through it, but it's going to take some time."

Brian Duperreault

A BEST

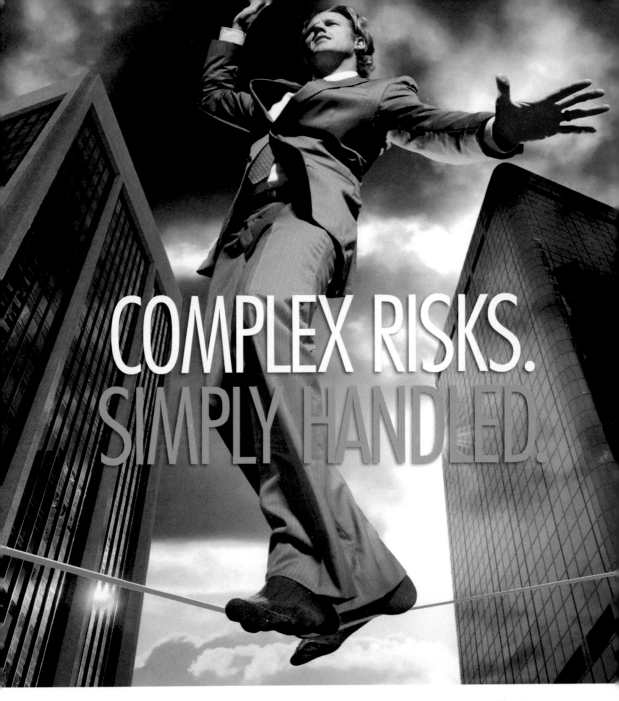

COMPLEX RISKS.
SIMPLY HANDLED.

Where there's risk, there's complexity. It's really that simple. We manage risk across a broad spectrum of niche industries. From social and human services, sports and fitness to entertainment, from education to the environment. At Philadelphia Insurance Companies, we handle complex risks and make them simple for you to manage.

Call 855.411.0797
or visit ThinkPHLY.com

A.M.Best A++ Rating

Ward's Top 50 2001-2016

96% Claims Satisfaction

100+ Niche Industries

PHILADELPHIA
INSURANCE COMPANIES

A Member of the Tokio Marine Group

Property/Casualty Market at a Glance

Property/casualty is known as "nonlife" insurance in many parts of the world. The word "property" usually refers to physical things, including autos, buildings, ships and other concrete items that can be lost, damaged or otherwise become a financial loss to the insured. The word "casualty" usually refers to the concept of liability, and is often associated with coverage of negligent acts or omissions. Casualty areas are some of the largest, including auto liability, professional liability, workers' compensation and general liability. The relative size of property/casualty insurers is often gauged by premiums collected.

In the United States, property/casualty insurers file a special statement with the National Association of Insurance Commissioners (NAIC). The filing is designed to determine premiums and losses by lines of business and to give an accurate view of the insurer's reserving for loss.

As of this publication, A.M. Best's database contained filing statements for 2,647 total single companies operating in the U.S. property/casualty market.

**U.S. Property/Casualty –
Top Insurers by Net Premiums Written (2015)**
(US$ billions)

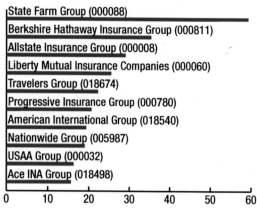

**U.S. Property/Casualty –
Top Insurers by Gross Premiums Written (2015)**
(US$ billions)

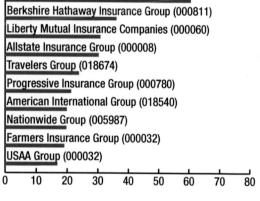

Source: BESTLINK – Best's Statement File – P/C, U.S.
Data as of June 14, 2016

According to the U.S. Department of Labor, 527,600 people work in the property/casualty industry.

According to A.M. Best's annual *Review & Preview* report, the property/casualty industry faces several issues:

Personal Lines

The personal lines segment, as well as the industry as a whole, continues to dedicate significant resources toward improving technologies, brand awareness and advertising. Companies are continuing to move away from legacy systems and install technology that improves and streamlines all facets of the insurance business. Companies of all shapes and sizes are undertaking these initiatives in an effort to

U.S. Property/Casualty –
Top Insurers by Total Admitted Assets (2015)
(US$ billions)

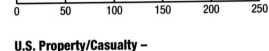

Berkshire Hathaway Insurance Group (000811)
State Farm Group (000088)
American International Group (018540)
Travelers Group (018674)
Liberty Mutual Insurance Companies (000060)
Nationwide Group (005987)
Allstate Insurance Group (000008)
CNA Insurance Companies (018313)
Hartford Insurance Group (000048)
USAA Group (004080)

0   50   100   150   200   250

U.S. Property/Casualty –
Top Insurers by Policyholder Surplus (2015)
(US$ billions)

Berkshire Hathaway Insurance Group (000811)
State Farm Group (000088)
American International Group (018540)
USAA Group (004080)
Travelers Group (018674)
Liberty Mutual Insurance Companies (000060)
Allstate Insurance Group (000008)
Hartford Insurance Group (000048)
Nationwide Group (005987)
Chubb Group of Insurance Companies (000012)

0   30   60   90   120   150

Source: BESTLINK – Best's Statement File – P/C, U.S.
Data as of June 15, 2016

U.S. Property/Casualty –
Direct Premiums Written
(US$ billions)

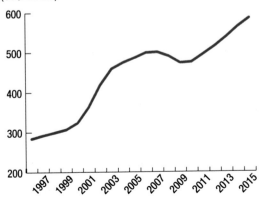

Source: BESTLINK – Aggregates & Averages
Property/Casualty United States & Canada, 2016 Edition

reduce expenses and maintain any possible competitive advantages. In addition, advertising continues to grow unabated, paced by the larger and well-known national carriers.

In addition to these technological initiatives, there is continued effort by companies to bundle personal lines products in order to deepen and enhance the customer relationship. Companies are also attracting customers as early as possible for their insurance needs; providing auto and renters policies to younger people can help establish a relationship that can eventually expand to homeowners, umbrella and other coverages as life circumstances dictate.

Auto
Auto writers have continued making investments to develop and improve tools used in data analytics and usage-based insurance. The penetration of usage-based insurance has increased in recent years, and more advanced pricing segmentation has been achieved as insurers can now better understand the unique driving characteristics of each insured. The larger auto writers have led the charge in this space, as they have and are willing to dedicate the necessary resources into the specific tools. Their efforts will likely enable them to continue attracting the most desirable business in the most sought-after risk categories.

Homeowners
Homeowners writers appear to continue to move toward a better understanding of risk and pricing, and less toward risk avoidance. Insurers are better able to pinpoint specific risks and more general geographic regions where they

believe they can operate profitably. A.M. Best believes those companies that have not been able to adapt to changing pricing and product parameters will have difficulty competing and will face possible adverse risk selection.

Commercial Lines

Commercial lines insurers have made significant strides in pricing sophistication to lessen the impact of the ebbs and flows of the pricing cycle on earnings. Commercial lines insurers' balance sheets and the levels of capitalization maintained by many insurers remain strong even after giving consideration to moderately underfunded reserves for the entirety of the sector.

Property/Casualty Coverage Types And Lines of Business

Property insurance covers damages or loss of property. As a result, rates can be significantly higher in areas susceptible to perils such as hurricanes. Casualty insurance covers indemnity losses and legal expenses from losses such as bodily injury or damage that the policyholder may cause to others.

Insurance companies set a reserve amount through a prediction of estimated loss costs over a period of time. Unlike property reserves, which are mostly for specific types of events, casualty reserves primarily cover events that may unfold well into the future (i.e., medical professional liability, workers' compensation, product liability and environmental-related claims). These "long-tail" lines of business are so named because of the length of time that may elapse before claims are finally settled.

Determining and comparing profitability among property/casualty companies typically is achieved through the combined ratio, which measures the percentage of claims and expenses incurred relative to premiums earned/written. A combined ratio of less than 100 means that the insurer is making an underwriting profit. Companies with combined ratios over 100 still may earn a profit, however, because the ratio does not account for investment income.

Property/casualty insurance generally falls into two areas of concentration: personal and commercial lines.

The two largest product lines within the personal lines sector are auto insurance and homeowners insurance.

Commercial lines include insurance for businesses, professionals and commercial establishments. There are many more varieties of commercial lines products than personal lines. The largest two lines are workers' compensation and other liability.

U.S. Property/Casualty – Direct Premiums Written by Line of Business (2015)
(US$ thousands)

	No of Cos.	Direct Premiums Written
Fire	1,052	12,871,279
Allied Lines	972	11,392,368
Multi Peril Crop	41	9,808,636
Federal Flood	133	2,869,640
Private Crop	32	953,094
Farmowners Multiperil	230	4,086,904
Homeowners Multiperil	906	88,810,446
Comm. Multiperil-Non-Liability	805	25,271,952
Comm. Multiperil-Liability	740	14,419,431
Mortgage Guaranty	19	4,871,127
Ocean Marine	196	3,754,032
Inland Marine	1,069	20,488,253
Financial Guaranty	16	530,113
Medical Prof. Liability	337	9,195,726
Earthquake	540	2,890,236
Group Accident & Health	105	4,351,866
Credit Accident & Health	11	171,106
Other Accident & Health	91	1,599,195
Workers' Comp.	713	54,522,916
Other Liability-Occ	1,313	39,561,470
Other Liability-Claims-Made	596	21,289,771
Excess WC	61	1,175,491
Products Liability	485	3,663,501
Private Pass Auto Liability	876	119,159,752
Commercial Auto Liability	878	23,766,366
Private Pass Auto Physical Damage	876	80,130,453
Commercial Auto Physical Damage	816	7,531,145
Aircraft	70	1,591,572
Fidelity	292	1,239,377
Surety	343	5,651,162
Burglary & Theft	419	282,020
Boiler & Mach	411	1,762,154
Credit	97	1,878,911
International	6	69,853
Warranty	65	2,801,989
Other Lines	129	1,393,037

Source: BESTLINK – Aggregates & Averages Property/Casualty U.S. & Canada, 2016 Edition

Personal Lines: Major Lines of Business

Personal insurance protects families, individuals and their property, typically homes and vehicles, from loss and damage. Auto and homeowners coverage dominates mostly because of legal provisions that mandate coverage be obtained.

The largest line of business in the property/casualty sector is auto insurance. According to A.M. Best's BestLink database, the top 50 groups writing auto insurance captured 87% of the total auto market, or $201 billion of the $230 billion market for all U.S. auto coverage. The largest writer of U.S. private passenger auto, and all auto coverage overall, remains State Farm Group.

Auto insurance includes collision, liability, comprehensive, personal injury protection and coverage in the event another motorist is uninsured or underinsured.

The second-largest line of personal property/casualty insurance is homeowners, representing approximately $86 billion in direct premiums written for the U.S. property/casualty industry. Historically, the leading cause of U.S. insured catastrophe losses has been hurricanes and tropical storms, followed by severe thunderstorms and winter storms. The top 25 groups writing homeowners multiperil coverage represented 75% of the U.S. market for homeowners coverage, according to A.M. Best's BestLink database. The largest writer of homeowners multiperil coverage is also State Farm Group.

Commercial Lines of Business

Commercial insurance protects businesses, hospitals, governments, schools and other organizations from losses.

Two of the top lines for the commercial lines segment are workers' compensation and general liability.

Workers' Compensation: Insurers on behalf of employers pay benefits regardless of who is to blame for a work-related injury or accident, unless the employee was negligent. In return, the employee gives up the right to sue.

General Liability: General liability insurance protects business owners (the "insured") from the risks of liabilities imposed by lawsuits and similar claims. Liability insurance is designed to offer its insureds specific protection against third-party insurance claims; in other words, payment is not typically made to the insured, but rather to someone suffering loss who is not a party to the insurance contract. In general, damages caused by intentional acts are not covered under general liability insurance policies. When a claim is made, the insurance carrier has the duty to defend the insured.

Other major lines of business in the property/casualty commercial sector include:

Aircraft (all perils): Aircraft coverage is often excluded under standard commercial general liability forms. Coverage for aircraft liability loss exposure can include hull (physical damage) and medical payments coverages.

Allied Lines: Coverage for loss of or damage to real or personal property by reason other than fire. Losses from wind and hail, water (sprinkler, flood, rain), civil disorder and damage by aircraft or vehicles are included.

Boiler and Machinery: Coverage for damage to boilers, pressure vessels and machinery.

Burglary and Theft: Coverage to protect property from burglary, theft, forgery, counterfeiting, fraud and the like. Protection can include on- and off-premises exposure.

Commercial Auto: Coverage that protects against financial loss because of legal liability for injury to persons or damage to property of others caused by the insured's motor vehicle.

Commercial Multiple Peril: Commercial insurance coverage combining two or more property, liability and/or risk exposures.

Fidelity: Coverage for employee theft of money, securities or property, written with a per loss limit, a per employee limit or a per position limit. Employee dishonesty coverage is one of the key coverages provided in a commercial crime policy.

Financial Guaranty: Credit protection for investors in municipal bonds, commercial mortgage-backed securities and auto or student loans. Provides financial recourse in the event of a default on the bond or other instrument.

Fire: Coverage for loss of or damage to real or personal property due to fire or lightning. Losses from interruption of business and loss of other income from these sources are included.

Inland Marine: Coverage for goods in transit and goods, such as construction equipment, subject to frequent relocation.

Medical Professional Liability: Protects against failure to use due care and the standard of care expected from a doctor, dentist, nurse, hospital or other health-related organization. Covers bodily injury or property damage as well as liability for personal injury.

Mortgage Guaranty: Insurance against financial loss because of nonpayment of principal, interest and other amounts agreed to be paid under the terms of a note, bond or other evidence of indebtedness that is secured by real estate.

Multiple Peril Crop: Protects against losses caused by crop yields that are too low. This line was developed initially by the U.S. Department of Agriculture.

Ocean Marine: Provides protection for all types of oceangoing vessels and their cargo as well as legal liability of owners and shippers.

Products Liability: Protection against loss arising out of legal liability because of injury or damage resulting from the use of a product or the liability of a contractor after a job is completed.

Surety: The surety bond guarantees that the principal of a bond will perform its obligations.

Other Lines of Commercial Insurance

Surplus Lines

If property/casualty coverage isn't available from admitted insurers—those licensed by a state—it can be purchased from a nonadmitted carrier. Most surplus lines business is commercial lines, although there is some personal lines coverage, such as homeowners insurance in catastrophe-prone areas. As nonadmitted carriers, surplus lines insurers are free from some coverage and pricing requirements that apply to admitted insurers.

Generally, policies are written by surplus lines insurers because admitted carriers have elected not to provide coverage. The reasons vary but include the following:

Distressed Risks: The risk does not meet the guidelines of the standard market due to unfavorable attributes such as a history of frequent losses.

Unique Risks: The risk is so specialized or unusual that it falls outside of what the admitted insurer is comfortable writing.

High-Capacity Risks: The risk requires high insurance limits that may exceed the capacity of the standard market. These are very large exposures with equally high potential for loss, such as aviation liability insurance.

Title Insurance

Virtually every real estate transaction depends upon a title insurance company. While other types of insurance generally insure against losses caused by future events, title insurance covers claims based on past events that have caused a defect in the land title, brought on by reasons such as public-record errors, forgeries or incorrect marital statements.

Although it can be classified as a property/casualty line, title insurance stands on its own. Title industry insurers pay out far fewer claims than the typical property/casualty insurer. Property/casualty insurers charge premiums annually; title insurers charge a premium once. The length of the property/casualty contract is annual; the title coverage is for the length of the property ownership, at least.

Unlike property/casualty profit cycles, which depend on the supply of insurance in the market (known as capacity), title insurance cycles stem from the number of real estate transactions. Housing activity plays an essential part because title companies collect premiums after the largest component of their costs—operating expenses—have been incurred. Because general expenses incurred as part of the title-search process typically make up 85% or more of premium volume, title insurers, unlike other property/casualty insurers, have little available cash flow for investments.

Catastrophe Impact

While other exposures can affect insurers' solvency, no single event weakens overall policyholder security quicker than a catastrophe. History has shown that when catastrophes hit, failures among U.S. insurance companies increase, sometimes precipitously, affecting significant numbers of policyholders. A.M. Best's P/C impairment studies, based on data from 1969 to the present, have shown that the common denominator among failures of U.S. insurers is a diminished operating environment, often triggered by external factors affecting the industry's underwriting or investment results. Negative underwriting events in the form of major catastrophes often stress already vulnerable companies to the breaking point.

Historically, hurricanes and tropical storms represent the greatest share of U.S. insured catastrophe losses. Severe thunderstorms and tornados also cause considerable insured losses.

Developing Issues ... and Opportunities

Insurers warn that a gathering cloud of emerging liability and property risks could lead to claims and losses that rival the largest natural disasters. But new technology and business models are opening doors to expanded insurance coverages.

Examples of emerging risks include:

Cybersecurity: Data loss from hacking and taking control of driverless cars or large ships.

Earthquakes caused by fracking: Incidents in Oklahoma after fluid injection have regulators and insurers on alert for greater seismic activity.

Endocrine disruptors: Widely used substances such as BPA phthalates affecting hormone systems, causing birth defects, development disorders and cancer.

Pandemics: Zika virus giving rise to claims over birth abnormalities.

Traumatic brain injuries: Concussions caused by frequent head contact playing sports.

Post-traumatic stress disorder: Potential causes from a variety of sources including battlefield, crime, accidents and abuse.

Police use of force: A marked rise in complaints over bodily injury by law enforcement, often captured on camera.

Lesser risks include nanotechnology, genetically modified organisms (GMOs), cellphones, e-cigarettes and more.

Other risks include greater dependency on large vessels for transporting crude oil. Carriers are also troubled by the volatility of fuel being extracted from the Bakken oil deposits, Praedicat CEO Robert Reville said. "It's more dangerous than regular oil, so there is greater risk of explosion with derailment."

Not all risks involve claims. Some are threats to insurers' basic business models. The technology world has seen large increases in investments in startup companies aimed at disrupting portions of the insurance industry. Berkshire Hathaway Chairman and CEO Warren Buffett recently talked about his company's auto insurer, Geico, when addressing potential risks, saying, "At some point in the future—though not, in my view, for a long time—Geico's premium volume may shrink because of driverless cars."

Meanwhile, insurers are actively embracing new technology that allows for better underwriting and reporting on drivers and vehicles. Progressive has been deploying its driving monitoring technology, known as Snapshot, and has expanded it beyond devices and into phone apps. Newer versions differ in that they differentiate, for instance, whether a user is traveling in a plane, train or automobile, and whether the user is an auto driver or passenger. Looking at continually evolving vehicle technology to improve safety, former President and CEO Glenn Renwick allowed that rates in the long-term "may be headed for a reduction."

RLI, an insurer that built its name on replacement contact lenses, looks to technology for flexibility and speed. RLI is testing the digital waters by rolling out on-demand coverage. Its Track Day product offers insurance for drivers who want to test out their car—be it a Subaru, a Porsche or a classic car—on a race track. The product can be purchased online as one-day coverage or bundled into a multipack that covers six trips to the track.

"This is pay-as-you-go, on-demand, which is the way the world is going," RLI President Craig Kliethermes said. "I don't know that we're going to make a lot of money with it, but we're learning. This is an opportunity to combine technology with the pay-as-you-go type of purchase behavior."

Coverages Available

Cyber liability is a rapidly advancing area. Here are some of the more common cyber insurance policies currently available.

THIRD-PARTY COVERAGE

Insures against the liability of the insured to third parties (i.e., a person or entity other than the insured, including clients and governmental entities) as a result of a data breach, cyberattack or similar covered loss as defined in the policy. Third-party cyber insurance coverage typically covers loss for steps the insured must take as a result of a data breach or cyberattack, including providing notice to customers or clients whose personal information has been stolen, credit monitoring for affected customers or clients, damages resulting from misuse of personal information of customers or clients, public relations expenses and litigation, including shareholder derivative actions and regulatory costs.

Sources: G. Richard Dodge Jr. and James Woods, partners in Mayer Brown's Insurance Industry Group

Regulatory Defense Expenses
Pays for defense costs of regulatory action due to breach of privacy regulation. Coverages may include fines and penalties.

Errors and Omissions
Protects a business when it causes damage to another company's network or IT system due to accidents or negligent errors.

Communications and Media Liability
Covers the risks of a company accidentally or negligently damaging another company's digital assets, intellectual property and artwork.

Network Security
Pays for data breach claims caused by failure to protect and monitor an IT system for viruses and malicious code entering a network. Claims can include expense to notify affected individuals of the breach and legal and forensic costs to determine the extent of the breach and how best to respond.

FIRST-PARTY COVERAGE

Insures against loss or damage sustained by the insured (i.e., the named policyholder) as a result of a data breach, cyberattack or similar covered loss as defined in the policy. First-party cyber insurance coverage typically covers the insured for damages directly resulting from a data breach or cyberattack, including compensation for loss of business, loss of data that was stolen, damage to the insured's digital content, cost of replacement of the insured's equipment damaged in an attack, damage to company brand and reputation, incident response and remediation including investigation and security audit expenses, and damage resulting from theft and extortion.

Sources: G. Richard Dodge Jr. and James Woods, partners in Mayer Brown's Insurance Industry Group

Extortion Threat
Coverage is available for cyberextortion, often as an add-on module to a cyber policy and sometimes as an enhancement to a kidnap and ransom policy. It covers the amount of the ransom (up to a sublimit) and, with negotiation, can include full limits for forensics investigations and remediation.

Crisis Management Expenses
Offers coverage for costs and expenses associated with managing a privacy breach, which may include forensic investigation expenses, call center, credit monitoring and public relations costs.

Software and Data Recovery Expenses
Pays for expenses to restore information/data after a failure of the computer system or network leading to destruction, corruption or loss of electronic information assets and/or data.

Computer Fraud
Coverage for loss of securities or money stolen by hackers from IT systems.

Business Interruption
When a company's computer system fails or there is a breach of network security by hackers or other attacks that lead to income loss, this coverage reimburses for profits lost during the attack.

Regulatory Defense Expenses
Pays for defense costs of regulatory action due to breach of privacy regulation. Coverages may include fines and penalties.

Sources: CRO Forum, Aon Risk Solutions, Hanover Insurance Co., IDT 911, Erie Insurance, Philadelphia Insurance Companies

BEST

Spotlight: Hands Off the Wheel

It's no longer a question of if we'll ever have self-driving cars. It's now a matter of when autonomous vehicles will become so commonplace that they will transform society in general and the insurance industry in particular.

"That's the million-dollar question these days," said Rob Slingerland, chief executive officer of online insurance marketer Answer Financial. "I don't think anyone debates that it will have a material impact. The debate's more about, 'When and how long will that take?'"

McKinsey and Company forecasts that consumers will begin to adopt autonomous vehicles around 2020, and these vehicles will be the primary mode of transportation by 2050. Other research suggests the majority of cars will have driverless capabilities by 2025, according to Carsten Prussog, chief executive United Kingdom, Ireland, Netherlands, Nordics, Baltics, Russia at Munich Re. Slingerland, however, sees regulation stalling the transformation from a driver-led to driverless society.

"Do you have to have a steering wheel, not have a steering wheel? How is that going to get defined?" Slingerland said, listing possible questions that could slow the adoption of driveless vehicles.

Whether the technology is five or 25 years away, risk managers of large organizations don't report a sense of urgency, according to a Munich Re survey completed at the 2016 RIMS conference in San Diego.

"The majority of risk managers really

aren't doing anything to prepare their organizations for the coming adoption of autonomous vehicle technology," said Mike Scrudato senior vice president at Munich Re America. However, risk managers are concerned about cyber, he noted.

"If you think of the integration of cyberrisk and auto risk, typically those are separate buys," Scrudato said. "Most people don't correlate those two things. But as vehicles become more and more connected, more and more automated, we see the potential increase of cyber exposure with auto exposure."

Insurers will have no choice but be drafted into the auto revolution. "You have to embrace the technology," Paul Graf, senior vice president at Claims Service Corporation of America, said. "Driverless cars and autonomous cars—that's going to be a huge futuristic development that the whole industry's going to see that they also need to embrace."

Part of embracing the technology is preparing for a wider range of claims.

"There's still likely to be crashes with vehicles, no matter

Rob Slingerland

if people are driving them or if they're being driven autonomously," Scrudato said. "It's just a matter of how will the liability evolve, and how will new products have to evolve to match with those liabilities."

"The shift in the liability would go from the operator, which is what the premise of auto insurance is—to insure us against human error, to the manufacturer," said Martin Frappolli, senior director of knowledge resources at The Institutes.

The Institutes uses the term "streaming transportation" to describe the convergence of autonomous vehicles with ride hailing (Uber or Lyft) and car sharing (Zipcar, Car2Go). Named for the technology that has transformed music and television, streaming transportation is a simple term for possibly complex disruption to come.

"Immediately, one of the biggest predictions is the total number of cars on the road could be reduced by up to 90%," Frappolli said. "There are some more conservative estimates that say 60% or 70%. If that comes to pass, the immediate impact is on carmakers, car dealers, car repair shops, law enforcement. If the number of accidents drops a lot, that's going to affect medical care, and all in a good way."

Still, many of today's basic comprehensive risks will remain, Slingerland said.

"Hail storms are still going to come that'll damage the car," Slingerland said. "The windshield is still going to get cracked by the rock flying on the road. The tree can still fall over and crunch those cars. There are still going to be aspects of personal insurance that are going to be needed, but how it's going to be provided and consumed will undoubtedly change."

These issues have some auto writers at least acknowledging the autonomous elephant in the room.

"I think some of them are already taking into account that the future could be very different," Frappolli said. "Some have put it into their guidance that it could affect their future. There are opportunities, as well. Every change like this, we use the term disruptive, we hear that a lot. What it means is some jobs and some industries will be destroyed; others will be created. I think insurers want to make sure that they're not left sitting still and they end up as the next Kodak or Polaroid."

With safer cars come fewer claims. With fewer claims comes less likelihood of approval to raise premium rates. With lower premium rates come lower profits. But with lower claims come lower payouts.

"I'm fascinated," Frappolli said. "I'm also comforted to know that by the time I'm no longer able to operate a vehicle, the vehicle will be able to do it on my behalf."

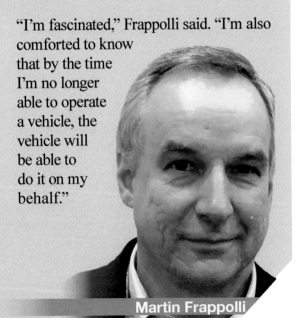

Martin Frappolli

Life Market at a Glance

Life/health insurers cover the risks of dying, offer retirement savings products and provide a variety of protections against disability, specific types of illness and more. As of this publication, A.M. Best's database contained annual filings for 1,832 single combined life/health companies operating in the United States. According to the U.S. Department of Labor, 334,900 people work in the U.S. life insurance sector. Life insurers often have longer investment and coverage horizons because retirement and mortality are often events that are decades away. The relative size of life/health insurers is often gauged by assets under management. Life insurers have increasingly embraced annuities and other forms of retirement savings. That's because sales of traditional life products have been flat or grown modestly. America's once-largest demographic group, baby boomers, is transitioning into retirement.

Top 10 U.S. Life/Health Companies
Ranked by 2015 Gross Premiums Written
(as of June 9, 2016)
(US$ thousands)

Rank	Company Name	AMB#	GPW
1	Metropolitan Life Insurance Company	006704	89,872,078
2	Kaiser Foundation Health Plan Inc	064585	56,745,870
3	Prudential Legacy Insurance Company NJ	060729	55,309,026
4	UnitedHealthcare Insurance Company	008290	42,124,683
5	Prudential Insurance Co of America	006974	31,799,749
6	Health Care Svc Corp Mut Legal Reserve	009193	31,264,775
7	New York Life Insurance Company	006820	29,966,947
8	MetLife Insurance Company USA	007330	27,395,346
9	Massachusetts Mutual Life Insurance Co	006695	26,513,191
10	Jackson National Life Insurance Company	006596	26,061,676

Top 10 U.S. Life/Health Companies
Ranked by 2015 Net Premiums Written
(as of June 9, 2016)
(US$ thousands)

Rank	Company Name	AMB#	NPW
1	Kaiser Foundation Health Plan Inc	064585	56,745,870
2	Prudential Legacy Insurance Company NJ	060729	55,309,026
3	UnitedHealthcare Insurance Company	008290	41,950,192
4	Health Care Svc Corp Mut Legal Reserve	009193	31,162,705
5	Metropolitan Life Insurance Company	006704	28,388,553
6	Jackson National Life Insurance Company	006596	23,650,556
7	Humana Insurance Company	007574	23,048,895
8	Massachusetts Mutual Life Insurance Co	006695	21,530,383
9	New York Life Insurance Company	006820	20,398,286
10	Lincoln National Life Insurance Co	006664	19,605,348

Top 10 U.S. Life/Health Companies
Ranked by 2015 Total Admitted Assets
(as of June 9, 2016)
(US$ thousands)

Rank	Company Name	AMB#	Admitted Assets
1	Metropolitan Life Insurance Company	006704	390,842,696
2	Teachers Insurance & Ann Assn of America	007112	270,094,422
3	Prudential Insurance Co of America	006974	244,995,697
4	Northwestern Mutual Life Ins Co	006845	238,543,832
5	John Hancock Life Insurance Company USA	006681	227,843,142
6	Lincoln National Life Insurance Co	006664	213,891,333
7	Massachusetts Mutual Life Insurance Co	006695	210,358,711
8	Jackson National Life Insurance Company	006596	189,096,800
9	MetLife Insurance Company USA	007330	173,761,514
10	American General Life Insurance Company	006058	166,711,283

Top 10 U.S. Life/Health Companies
Ranked by 2015 Capital & Surplus
(as of June 9, 2016)
(US$ thousands)

Rank	Company Name	AMB#	Capital & Surplus
1	Teachers Insurance & Ann Assn of America	007112	34,735,498
2	Kaiser Foundation Health Plan Inc	064585	24,896,991
3	Northwestern Mutual Life Ins Co	006845	19,659,624
4	New York Life Insurance Company	006820	19,495,935
5	Massachusetts Mutual Life Insurance Co	006695	14,982,532
6	Metropolitan Life Insurance Company	006704	14,484,993
7	Prudential Insurance Co of America	006974	11,543,730
8	American Family Lf Assur Co of Columbus	006051	11,297,855
9	State Farm Life Insurance Company	007080	9,559,920
10	Health Care Svc Corp Mut Legal Reserve	009193	9,444,954

Source: BESTLINK, A.M. Best data.

The U.S. life/health industry collected more than $647 billion in premium income and had $6.5 trillion in assets as of 2015, the most recent full year available. The largest lines of business as measured by premium income, in order, are individual annuities, group annuities and ordinary life. Other lines of business include supplemental contracts, credit life, group life, industrial life, group accident & health, credit accident & health and other accident & health.

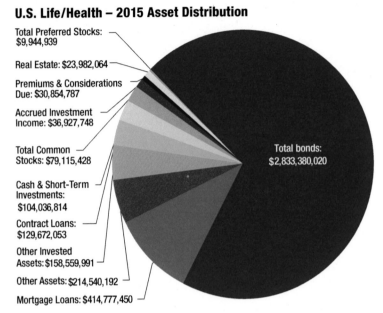

U.S. Life/Health – 2015 Asset Distribution

Total Preferred Stocks: $9,944,939

Real Estate: $23,982,064

Premiums & Considerations Due: $30,854,787

Accrued Investment Income: $36,927,748

Total Common Stocks: $79,115,428

Cash & Short-Term Investments: $104,036,814

Contract Loans: $129,672,053

Other Invested Assets: $158,559,991

Other Assets: $214,540,192

Mortgage Loans: $414,777,450

Total bonds: $2,833,380,020

Source: **BESTLINK** – *Aggregates & Averages Life/Health U.S. & Canada 2016 Edition* Securities are reported on the basis prescribed by the National Association of Insurance Commissioners.

According to the 2016 edition of *Best's Key Rating Guide - Life/Health, United States and Canada*, Metropolitan Life Insurance Co. leads the list of largest life/health companies ranked by total admitted assets, with $391 billion in total admitted assets as of year-end 2015.

Risk Profile

The risk profile of life insurance is very different from that of property/casualty insurance. Life insurance is generally more asset intensive, and most product liabilities have a substantially longer duration.

The main purpose of life insurance is to cover the risk of dying too early or, in the case of annuities, the risks that may come with living longer than expected. Policies help beneficiaries maintain their standard of living after the policyholder dies. They also can protect beneficiaries and insureds from the possibility of outliving their assets.

While some types of life insurance include a savings component that can provide retirement income, life insurance itself isn't necessarily an investment. But for insurance companies, and especially life insurers, profitability is largely dependent on investment performance. In general, life insurers have enough data surrounding life expectancies and risk classes to determine rates and to accurately predict claims.

Because a policy can remain in effect for decades, life insurers' obligations tend to be relatively long-term. As a result, many insurers invest in longer-duration assets such as long-term bonds and real estate. The current low interest rate environment has put increased pressure on life insurers' investment portfolios.

Important Lines of Life Business and Products

Life insurers market a variety of life products that range from simple to complex.

Total Life, In Force & Issued: The size of a life company can be measured by the face amount of its portfolio — that is, the amount of life insurance it has issued as well as the amount in force. In force is the total face amount of insurance outstanding at a point in time. Issued measures the face amount of policies an insurer has sold within a given time period.

Permanent Life: Permanent life provides death benefits and cash value in return for periodic payments. Cash surrender value, or nonforfeiture value, is the sum of money an insurance company will pay a policyholder if he or she decides to cancel the policy before it expires or before he or she dies. Over the long term, these products usually produce solid, sustainable profitability that is derived from adequate pricing, underwriting and investment returns. Permanent life products include whole life, universal life and variable universal life.

Whole Life: Pays a death benefit and also accumulates a cash value. These have a high initial expense strain for the issuing company due to large first-year commissions to agents as a percentage of premiums. Over time, whole life provides an income stream to the company and the agent. It carries premium, death benefit and cash value guarantees that other products don't provide.

Universal Life: These are flexible premium policies that incorporate a savings element. The cash values that are accumulated are put into investments with the intention of earning more in interest. Those accumulations can be used to reduce later premiums, or to build up the cash value. For companies offering this product, the premium payment flexibility adds an element of uncertainty, as does the potential for changing market conditions that can affect interest rates. The next generation of this product line, universal life with secondary guarantees, offers competitive rates while providing long-term premium and death benefit guarantees, regardless of actual performance. The tight pricing and high reserve requirements can limit profitability.

Variable Universal Life: These flexible premium policies allow for investments of the cash value into mutual-fund-like accounts the insurance carrier holds in separate accounts rather than in its general account. Because policy values will vary based on the performance of investments, these policies present an investment risk to the policyholder. Rather than having a monthly addition to the cash value based upon a declared interest-crediting rate, the accumulated cash value of the variable policy is adjusted daily to reflect the investment experience of the funds selected. Insurers can be susceptible to

EXPECT BIG THINGS®
FROM APPLIED UNDERWRITERS

Expect big things in workers' compensation. Expect to save a third of your clients 30% or more. Most classes approved, nationwide. For information call (877) 234-4450 or visit auw.com/us. Follow us at bigdoghq.com.

APPLIED®
UNDERWRITERS

profit fluctuations because of the equity market's effect on mutual fund fees. In addition, the insurer lacks control over separate-account assets, and policyholder behavior may impact profitability.

Term Life: Provides protection for a specified period of time. It pays a benefit only if the insured's death occurs during the coverage period. It can be considered a pure protection product and a consumer's entry-level life insurance product. Term periods typically range from one year to 30 years, although there are annually renewable policies, which are designed for longer durations. Term life, which is a highly competitive product, is marketed through many traditional distribution channels, as well as through financial institutions, banks and various direct distribution channels including the internet. More recent products offer long-term premium guarantees, where the premium is guaranteed to be the same for a given period of years. Return of premium (ROP) term products have also become popular of late, offering policyowners a refund of all premiums paid if the insured is still alive at the end of the term period. Concerns to insurers include high lapse rates, compressed margins and high reserve requirements.

Group Life: Generally in the form of term life, group life is marketed to employers or association groups. The cost also may be shared by the participant and the master policyholder, usually the employee and employer, respectively. Typically, an initial benefit level may be paid by the employer, and in some cases, employees may elect to pay for additional coverage. Like with term life, competition is intense.

Annuity Products

Insurance companies provide annuities, which at their most basic are contracts that ensure an income stream. A payment or series of payments is made to an insurance company, and in return, the insurer agrees to pay an income for a specified time period. Annuities can take many forms but have a couple of basic properties: an immediate or deferred payout with fixed (guaranteed) or variable returns. Consequently, different annuity types can resemble certificates of deposit, pensions or even investment portfolios.

Challenges to the Annuity Industry

Life insurance companies must minimize the risk of disintermediation. This happens when deferred annuity holders seeking higher-yielding alternatives withdraw funds prematurely (often during periods of increasing interest rates), and force companies to pay these surrenders by liquidating investments that may be in an unrealized loss position. Insurers can mitigate this risk by matching the duration of its interest-sensitive liability portfolio with the duration of its asset portfolio, and by selling a diversified portfolio of products. Insurers also mitigate risk by designing deferred annuities with market-value adjustments on surrender values.

Immediate Annuities: These annuities are designed to guarantee owners a pre-determined income stream on a monthly, quarterly, semiannual or annual basis in exchange for a lump sum. Options are limited from the annuity holder's perspective, so profits are generally less volatile in the short term. However, the long-term nature of these products exposes the insurer to reinvestment risk and longevity risk.

Group Annuities: These differ slightly from individual annuities in that the payout is dependent upon the life expectancy of all the members of the group rather than on the individual. Many company retirement plans, such as 401(k) plans, are annuities that will pay a regular income to the retiree. Tax-deferred annuity plans—403(b) and 457 plans—also are used widely by public-sector and nonprofit workers.

Deferred Annuities: A type of long-term savings product that allows assets to grow tax-deferred until annuitization. This product category includes:

Traditional Fixed Annuities: These products guarantee a minimum rate of interest during the time the account is growing, and typically guarantee a minimum benefit upon annuitization

For the issuer, fixed annuities are subject to significant asset/liability mismatch risks, as described above. Also, when interest rates fall, spread earnings—or the difference between the yield on investments and credited rates—can decrease, and asset cash flows must be reinvested at lower rates.

Fixed-Indexed Annuities: These products are credited with a return that is based on changes in an equity index. The insurance company typically guarantees a minimum return. Payouts may be periodic or in a lump sum. The potential for gains is an attractive feature during favorable market conditions; however, gains may not be as favorable as those available from variable annuities or straight equity investments. Sales of these products may decline if equity markets go through a prolonged downturn or a prolonged upturn.

Variable Annuities: The participant is given a range of investment options, typically mutual funds, from which to choose. The rate of return on the purchase payment, and the amount of the periodic payments, will vary depending on the performance of the selected investments and the level of expense charges in the product.

Variable annuity sales tend to slump during unfavorable equity market conditions. In addition, the primary sources of revenue for these products are account-value-based fees, which also decline when market conditions deteriorate. Relatively thin margins, increasing product complexity (e.g., guaranteed living benefits) and volatile capital requirements put variable annuities at the riskier end of the product continuum, from the standpoint of the issuing insurer.

Because variable annuities allow for investments in equity and fixed-income securities, they are regulated by the U.S. Securities and Exchange Commission. Fixed annuities and fixed-indexed annuities are not securities, and as such, are not regulated by the SEC.

Accident & Health Products

Credit Accident & Health: This insurance covers a borrower for accidental injury, disability and related health expenses. It is designed specifically to make monthly payments until the insured can recover and resume earning income. If an individual is totally disabled for the life of the loan, the policy would pay the remaining balance, in most cases, but only one month at a time.

Group Accident & Health: These plans are designed for a natural group, such as employees of a single employer, or union members, and their dependents. Insurance is provided under a single policy, with individual certificates issued to each participant.

Other Accident & Health: Products that fall into this category could be policies for individuals that cover major medical, disability insurance, long-term care, dental, dread disease or auxiliary coverages such as Medicare supplement.

Life Insurers Search for New Models, Technology

A.M. Best's annual *Review & Preview* report details a range of issues facing the life/annuity sectors.

There is a heightened sense of urgency for owners, shareholders and policyholders to ensure companies are not continually increasing risks. However, due to prolonged slow growth in many traditional products and ongoing lack of earnings lift from the financial markets in terms of low interest rates and higher equity volatility, many insurers are reaching for new business and higher returns often associated with higher risk—although they currently maintain ample levels of risk-based capital.

Ongoing challenges remain:

- Historically low long-term interest rates.
- Marginal to declining premium growth in traditional business lines.
- Regulatory uncertainty around accounting and capital/reserving issues.
- Bringing forward an antiquated business model with increasing technological costs.
- Updating distribution models to meet varied population cohorts.
- Continued drag and subpar performance from legacy lines of business.

On top of these challenges, A.M. Best recognizes some new challenges:

- The aggregation of longevity exposure from increasing life expectancy trends.
- Enterprise risk management and the rise of cyberrisk as a life catastrophe event.
- Retooling of the underwriting process with improved data mining and predictive modeling.
- Increasing investment risk from traditional and nontraditional asset classes.
- Changing regulatory landscape focusing on sales suitability practices.
- Favorable M&A conditions, including new underlying drivers of increased activity.
- Increased competition, including nontraditional players.

The economy continues to pressure not only investment portfolio returns but the profitability of many products, both spread-based and those with underlying long-term interest rate assumptions. In addition, although the industry maintains minimal investment exposure to equities, such products with equity components are either less popular or increasingly costly to hedge.

What has become a bigger issue for the industry is the antiquated business model from the point of sale through the back-office administration of the business. Underwriting-specific areas—such as data management, customer segmentation and distribution models—need a makeover to remain competitive, particularly with more nimble and technology-friendly new entrants. In particular, companies are struggling with developing simplified products and the means of reaching potential policyholders without disrupting existing channels. To date, the middle markets, non-English-speaking segments and most millennials remain underserved in the life/annuity industry.

Developing Issues

Life insurance sales generally remain challenging with weak organic growth in certain lines of business due to the mature nature of the industry. With the exception of indexed universal life and whole life insurance, life sales have been modest. Sales of indexed UL and fixed-indexed annuities have grown in popularity with increasing levels of competition as companies add these products to their existing platforms. Increased pricing, low interest rates and limited consumer interest have pushed life insurance ownership to 30-year lows.

Top line sales growth for the industry was modest in 2015. There was some modest growth within the ordinary and group life sectors due to strong demand for indexed universal life and whole life products. Within the annuity sector gowth was driven primarily by fixed-indexed annuities and pension risk transfer group annuities.

The industry has been focused on retirement products for growth, with individual annuity sales continuing to be strong for the industry and remaining the largest contributor to premiums and pretax operating gains. The variable annuity market has gradually shifted over the past few years, away from equity market and guarantee risk and toward investment-only variable annuities.

Spotlight: Health and Wellness

The cost of treating sick policyholders has prompted many insurers to increasingly focus on promoting wellness. The issue is particularly acute in Asia, where rising economies have offered residents the opportunity to pursue behaviors such as smoking, poor diets and sedentary lifestyles.

"What are we really seeing? We're seeing people getting sicker," said Mark Saunders, group chief strategy and corporate development officer, AIA. "If you know the statistics, three main lifestyle choices, which can be smoking, bad diet, lack of exercise, lead to four major diseases—cancer, diabetes, lung disease, heart disease—which create 50% of the deaths worldwide and 80% of the disease burden. That's coming to Asia and coming to Asia now.

"One of the big changes we're seeing throughout our industry is increased focus around wellness and health," Saunders added. "Companies like AIA introducing wellness programs, trying to encourage people to change their behavior through lifestyle. We help them know their health. We help them improve their health.

"Then we reward them for doing that through either enhanced benefits on their life insurance policy or some other gifts and things that will encourage them to change their long-term behavior and therefore change the risk, leading to healthier societies, better economies—better for our customers and better for our business."

Another threat to client wellness is disease, with global outbreaks of special concern to some.

"If we're talking about something with a very high mortality and morbidity event, one of the things that people usually worry about the most is something like an influenza event. It can go global," explained Doug Fullam, manager, life and health modeling, AIR Worldwide. "It's very hard for even the health care industry to do a ton. They can help provide fluids and different things like that, but it's not going to stop the transmission. It's going to spread to all corners of the world.

"That's one of the ones that we worry about," Fullam said. "You might hear from your local government, whether state or federal

Mark Saunders

Doug Fullam

level—even if we're talking about a different country—talk about the next flu pandemic.

"Alternatively, there are some things that are circulating right now," Fullam said. "We have Middle Eastern Respiratory Syndrome, MERS. It's circulating in Saudi Arabia. That may become a pandemic if it breaks out of that area. Also, we do have Zika that's going on right now. That one, people are not as worried about it. I actually am more worried about MERS, but Zika's also out there and potentially could become a pandemic or at least a large epidemic."

Health Market at a Glance

Health insurers focus principally on providing health coverage and related protection products. A.M. Best's database contained annual filing information for 1,038 single health insurance companies in the United States. According to the U.S. Department of Labor, more than 547,000 people worked in the health insurance industry in 2016.

Health insurers typically have shorter investment horizons than life insurers or property/casualty insurers that focus on liability coverage. Health insurers are measured by premiums and membership in their programs, sometimes known as "covered lives."

Health Insurance Coverage of the U.S. Population – 2015

Military 2%
Individual 7%
No insurance 9%
Covered by employer-sponsored health insurance 49%
Covered by Medicare 14%
Covered by Medicaid 20%

Source: Kaiser Family Foundation, State Health Facts

A report by the Kaiser Family Foundation estimates that in 2015, 49% of the U.S. population was covered by employer-sponsored health insurance. Another 20% was covered by Medicaid, a state-based program for those of limited financial means. Another 14% of the population was covered by Medicare, which is designed for seniors. About 9% of the U.S. population has no insurance, Kaiser estimates. Individuals account for 7% of the population covered followed by 2% of the military.

Health insurance policies pay benefits to insureds who become ill or injured. Managed care is the most common form of coverage. In managed care, insurance companies establish fee agreements with doctors and hospitals to provide health care services. If managed care health insurance is provided through employment, the employer pays the managed care plan a set amount of money in advance for all health care costs. The employee may have to contribute a portion of the premium to the employer via a payroll deduction. The employee then pays a flat amount for the services as either a copayment or a percentage of the cost of services provided.

In most managed care plans, doctors or hospitals are chosen from a network of providers. Some managed care plans allow for visits to doctors outside the network, at a greater cost to the employee.

Some of the largest carriers of health insurance are Blue Cross Blue Shield plans and publicly traded companies. Blue Cross Blue Shield companies operate independently as part of an association. Blue Cross companies originally focused on hospitalization coverage. Blue Shield companies originally focused on coverage for doctor visits. The two associations have since merged and now provide health insurance coverage options for employer groups and individuals.

Health Insurer Entity Types

Major types of health plans include:

HMO (Health Maintenance Organization): Employees select a primary care physician, who oversees all aspects of the employee's medical care and provides referrals to see specialists. Most services received from doctors or hospitals out of the plan's network are not covered.

PPO (Preferred Provider Organization): A network of doctors, hospitals and other health care providers make up the organization, but the PPO also allows an employee to go to specialists, out-of-network doctors or hospitals without needing prior authorization from a primary care physician. However, more of the costs to receive care outside the network are shouldered by the employee.

POS (Point of Service): The employee must designate a primary care physician but retains the option to receive services from doctors without a referral or go outside the network for care and shoulder much of the cost.

Fee-for-service health plans, or indemnity plans, were once the traditional route for coverage. There is no network of pre-approved providers, so an employee can choose to visit any doctor or hospital. These plans cost the most and have dwindled sharply in the past 30 years.

Some employers offer plans that combine a pretax savings account with a high-deductible health plan (HDHP) to establish a health savings account (HSA). The HSA pays for qualified and routine health care expenses with tax-free money until the deductible is met; then the insurance coverage takes over. The funds in the HSA also can be used for expenses the HDHP doesn't cover, and HSA balances carry forward to future years.

Consolidated membership and revenue growth for group health insurance has been limited, since employers have reduced head count as companies look to manage expenses.

In addition, the price of health coverage has become a focal point when employers look to provide coverage for their employees. Many employers have implemented benefit modifications to lower the impact of premium rate increases at renewal.

Products and Terms

Health products come in a wide variety of forms and address basic health needs, ranging from medical care to specialized forms of illness and accident coverage. Health products include:

Indemnity Health Plans: These may be offered on an individual or group basis. Indemnity plans allow members to choose their own doctor or hospital. The carrier then pays a fixed portion of total charges. Indemnity plans are often known as "fee-for-service" plans.

High-Deductible Health Plans: These may feature low premiums and an integrated deductible for both medical and pharmacy costs. Some plans combine a health plan with a Health Savings Account.

Health Savings Accounts: Participants may contribute pretax money to be used for qualified medical expenses. HSAs, which are portable, must be linked to a high-deductible health insurance policy.

Health Reimbursement Arrangements: HRAs are available to high-deductible health plan owners who are not qualified for health savings accounts.

Qualified High-Deductible Health Plans: These have lower premiums and cover health care expenses only after the insured has paid each year a large amount out of pocket. To qualify as a health plan coupled with a Health Savings Account, the Internal Revenue Code requires the deductible to be at least $1,300 for an individual and $2,600 for a family, with a maximum annual deductible and other out of pocket expenses of $6,550 for an individual and $13,100 for a family.

Dental Plans: Traditional dental plans may help cover preventive, basic and major services.

Dental Preferred Provider Organizations: These offer discounts to members who use in-network dental providers.

Vision Plans: Vision care plans may cover regular eye exams, treatment for conditions and assistance with corrective lenses.

Pharmacy: Plans may cover part or all of prescription drug costs.

Flexible Spending Account (FSA): This pays for additional services and costs that the primary health plan may not cover.

Medicare Advantage: This provides Medicare-eligible retirees the benefits of

Medicare, plus additional features and benefits such as wellness programs and case management services.

Common health insurance terms include:

Coinsurance: For health insurance, it is a percentage of each claim above the deductible paid by the policyholder. For a 20% health insurance coinsurance clause, the policyholder pays for the deductible plus 20% of covered losses. After paying 80% of losses up to a specified ceiling, the insurer starts paying 100% of losses.

Copayment: A predetermined, flat fee an individual pays for health care services, in addition to what insurance covers. For example, some HMOs require a $20 copayment for each office visit, regardless of the type or level of services provided during the visit. Copayments are not usually specified by percentages.

Disease Management: A system of coordinated health care interventions and communications for patients with certain medical conditions.

Developing Issues

According to A.M. Best's annual *Review & Preview* report on the U.S. health insurance sector, insurers are adapting to a business landscape shaped as much by social and regulatory issues as it is by competition.

Health insurers are looking at initiatives to better control the cost of care, which includes disease management programs and better coordination of care. As a result, there has been increased collaboration with providers, and that can benefit all parties, including the patient. Health insurers are able to give providers data that can be used to monitor patients and help ensure that proper treatment is obtained. This is particularly important for higher risk individuals, as lack of appropriate treatment could lead to deterioration of the medical condition and potential hospitalization.

Changing the Customer Experience

In response to the continuing evolution of the health insurance marketplace, health insurers are paying careful attention to the customer experience. This change in focus is being driven by several factors, including a shift in the health insurance purchase from the employer to the individual consumer, as well as the presence of millennials, who have different needs. Furthermore, with the implementation of the Patient Protection and Affordable Care Act (PPACA) and exchange products, some purchasers are viewing health insurance as a commoditized product where price can be the determining factor. As a result, carriers are trying to find a way to differentiate themselves and meet the needs of different groups of customers.

Millennials are a big challenge because they approach health care and health insurance in an entirely different way than their parents or grandparents. Often called "young invincibles," this age group does not see the value in health insurance, mostly due to being young and healthy. Additionally, under a provision of the PPACA, they are allowed to remain on their parents' policies until age 26, so they do not need to be active participants in the selection of their health insurance until they age out. These younger generation purchasers are interested in plans that give them choice, flexibility and ease of use, with an emphasis on quality and value. Millennials look for convenience in a health plan and in access to health care. These individuals prefer to access information through an app, ask customer service representatives questions through an online chat, locate retail clinics in their network via the internet, and utilize telemedicine. Additionally, millennials are highly likely to look at customer comments or reviews on the web, so public perception of an insurer is important.

In addition, many carriers are adopting a model in which the member is at the center of all operating activities and business strategies, with special attention to satisfaction metrics. High levels of customer satisfaction can result in better retention rates and medical compliance. Plans are collecting data, including customer feedback, to perform analysis geared toward measuring how well they are reaching customer expectations. Some carriers are also analyzing customer service inquiries to understand the primary reason for these contacts, to better address member concerns and to improve operations so customer service is increased and the need for inquiries is decreased.

Health carriers are creating additional avenues for consumer engagement and expanding member access to information. The mindset is for health plans to make available consumer-desired access points, whether it is communication in a specific language, in-person interaction or use of different media such as phone, web, email and mobile technology. Furthermore, consumers want plans that are easy to purchase, understand and use. Plan designs that include deductibles, co-insurance, different
in- and out-of-network coverage, as well as out-of-pocket maximums, can be confusing.

Insurers are utilizing data analytics to personalize member communications regarding their health plan and care. They are also making available transparency tools, including cost estimators and provider quality data. In the internet age, consumers are used to being able to do cost comparison and look up reviews or ratings to be able to make informed decisions when they make purchases.

Spotlight: A New Team Takes the Field

As baby boomers beat a hasty retreat from the workforce, all eyes—and many resources—are on young adults who might never have considered insurance as a career.

"Some people perceive the insurance industry as a dinosaur, a very mature industry that's not cutting-edge," Marsh USA Managing Director Roger Fell said.

"One of the things we're trying to do is educate the younger folks, Generation Y, the millennials, about all the various opportunities in insurance," said Kevin O'Brien, CEO of Inland Marine Underwriters Association. "It's brokers to loss control to actuaries. These are things that young people really aren't that familiar with. They think of insurance as the life insurance salesman with the patent leather shoes."

Even those who opt for an insurance career can vex employers, who notice age isn't the only thing separating junior employees from their senior counterparts.

"There have definitely been challenges between the more seasoned workers and the people newer to the game," Tina Lehman, marketing manager for Eberl Claims Service, said. "Different learning styles, different management styles—all that needs to be incorporated to continue to make everything successful."

Eberl's response?

"We like to keep it fresh," Lehman said. "We hire new people regularly. We do a lot of in-office training. We seek out-of-office training. We go to a lot of seminars so we can stay current on all the different styles out there. We make sure we're appealing to everyone, and also offering compensation packages and work-life balance packages that keep people interested and motivated for our company."

The Insurance Society of Philadelphia established NextGen, which welcomes and supports young professionals through networking, social, charitable and educational opportunities. "We have our own executive board that runs concurrently with the ISoP executive board, and they listen to everything we have to say," NextGen Vice Chair Denise Hunter said. "We have input on decisions from who

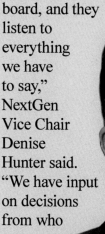

Tina Lehman

Kevin O'Brien

should get scholarships to how we should do our gala programs to what things we're going to do for I-Day."

The American Association of Managing General Agents reaches younger talent through targeted educational programs. University East and University West—held annually in different parts of the United States—provide information for everyone from beginners to experienced insurance professionals. Two boot camps—one for rookies; the other for those ready for more advanced underwriting training—also support newer employees.

In 2016, the AAMGA launched its Underwriting Certificate Program, available at existing risk management and insurance programs across the country.

"What we're trying to do is familiarize [RMI students] with the applications, manuals and all the different tools that you need in order to be an underwriter, because we can give them that head start when they enter the workforce," said Chip Pecchio, chair of the AAMGA Education Committee. "That's going to be a tremendous benefit. That certificate should help them land better jobs."

The AAMGA also sponsors a white-paper research competition for students, and actively recruits members for its Under Forty Organization.

"One of our big initiatives is education," UFO President Matt Lynch said. "Also networking; networking is very important to us. The people we meet in the Under Forty Organization are people we're going to be working with for the next 20 and 30 years. These

relationships are key to their success as they move forward."

Savvy recruiters recognize the younger generation has grown up with technology, which can be used to attract new hires.

Insure Learn, which develops online loss prevention training for managing general agents and carriers, embraces gaming. "We have a lot of younger people coming into the workforce. They grew up as gamers; they have a short attention span," Insure Learn President Steve Haws noted. "We just released an online trivia game where an employee can go in and in six minutes compete against other employees and learn something at the same time about how to be a safer employee in whatever their particular job is. We've got a couple other things that are on the burner right now that are going to move loss prevention into more of a social type of experience for the insureds."

"Technology and analytics will play a big role," agreed William Rosa, vice president at XL Catlin. "Insurance companies are becoming more analytical and much better with technology. I believe that will entice young people to join our industry."

Still, it often comes down to meeting

Denise Hunter

prospective employees where they are. "At Marsh we do a lot of recruiting out of the big risk management schools, and we have great success in getting good talent and retaining that talent," Fell said.

"A number of E&S carriers, Lloyd's and our partners and competitors around the country, are partnering with risk management programs at different universities, sponsoring E&S days where they go and spend a day speaking to the students," Hank

Hank Watkins

Watkins, president of Lloyd's North America, said. "They talk broadly about the insurance industry, but more specifically about how E&S can really be a focal point for their futures going forward."

"Ultimately it boils down to education and really creating an awareness of the opportunities, the structure, the players and the distribution piece of the specialty insurance realm," said Nick Abraham, a member of the AAMGA's UFO.

Nick Abraham

Overview of Reinsurance

Broadly put, reinsurance is insurance for insurers.

Insurance companies face many risks in their daily operations, including:

Asset risks, or the changing nature of investment values.

Credit risk, or the obligations owed by customers and/or debtors.

Liability risk, or potential losses due to inadequate pricing or reserving, or from catastrophes and other events.

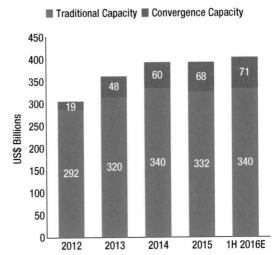

Estimated Dedicated Reinsurance Capital: 2012 to Midyear 2016

■ Traditional Capacity ■ Convergence Capacity

Sources: Guy Carpenter, A.M. Best data and research

Reinsurance is a transaction that indemnifies the primary insurer against those potential losses. The primary insurer, or ceding company, transfers a portion of risk to the reinsurer. How much risk and what conditions trigger the reinsurance are specified in the treaties. Generally, the primary carrier retains a fair amount of the risk.

Reinsurance allows insurers to increase the maximum amount they can insure. However, most reinsurance contracts do not absolve the ceding insurer's responsibility to pay the insurance claims should the reinsurer fail. The first reinsurance companies were born out of a major fire in 1842 that burned a large section of Hamburg, Germany, and killed at least 50 people. The conflagration exposed the inability of insurers to cope with such a catastrophe, and the insurers recognized the need to distribute risk portfolios among several carriers.

For a basic reinsurance scenario, take an office building worth $20 million. A primary carrier may accept the risk of loss and then turn to a reinsurer, agreeing to cover the first $10 million and ceding the rest. If losses at the building then were to exceed the primary layer of $10 million, say $14 million, the reinsurer would be called upon to cover the remaining $4 million.

In a case like this, the arrangement is said to be a nonproportional agreement, also known as an excess of loss agreement. In proportional agreements, the primary insurer and reinsurer share the liability risk proportionately. In the case of a quota share agreement, the primary insurer and reinsurer split the premiums and losses on a fixed percentage basis.

The two basic types of reinsurance arrangements are treaty and facultative. Treaty reinsurance contractually binds the insurer and reinsurer together, with respect to certain specified business. The treaty requires the insurer to cede all the risks specified by the agreement with the reinsurer, and the reinsurer must assume those specified risks. This means that the reinsurer automatically takes the risk for all policies that are covered by the treaty, and not just one particular policy.

Facultative reinsurance, on the other hand, is done more on a case-by-case basis. The reinsurance is issued after an individual analysis of the situation and by deciding coverage case by case. The reinsurer can determine if it wants some or all of the risk associated with that particular policy. This arrangement usually takes place when the

Top 25 Global Reinsurance Groups

Ranked by unaffiliated gross premium written in 2015.
(USD millions)[1]

| 2016 Ranking | Company Name | Reinsurance Premiums Written | | | | Total Shareholders' Funds[2] | Ratios[3] | | |
| | | Life & Non-Life | | Non-Life only | | | | | |
		Gross	Net	Gross	Net		Loss	Expense	Combined
1	Munich Reinsurance Company[4]	36,976	35,279	19,319	18,449	33,837	57.0	32.6	89.7
2	Swiss Re Ltd.	32,249	30,442	19,561	19,197	33,606	53.3	34.1	87.4
3	Hannover Rueckversicherung AG[4]	18,651	15,945	10,204	8,851	9,591	69.3	25.3	94.7
4	SCOR S.E.	14,665	13,228	6,254	5,584	6,953	59.1	32.0	91.1
5	Lloyd's [5,6]	12,740	10,237	12,740	10,237	35,903	48.7	38.0	86.7
6	Berkshire Hathaway Inc.[7]	12,236	12,236	7,049	7,049	258,627	N/A	N/A	90.5
7	Reinsurance Group of America Inc.	9,371	N/A	N/A	N/A	6,135	N/A	N/A	N/A
8	China Reinsurance (Group) Corporation	8,283	7,546	4,743	4,652	10,934	58.0	38.0	96.0
9	Everest Re Group Ltd.[8]	5,876	5,378	5,876	5,378	7,609	56.6	26.8	83.4
10	PartnerRe Ltd.	5,548	5,230	4,277	4,022	6,903	54.0	31.6	85.6
11	Korean Reinsurance Company	5,443	3,739	4,812	3,197	1,719	80.5	18.0	98.4
12	Great West Lifeco	4,173	4,065	N/A	N/A	18,220	N/A	N/A	N/A
13	Transatlantic Holdings, Inc	3,662	3,387	3,662	3,387	5,210	55.2	34.3	89.5
14	General Insurance Corporation of India[9]	2,786	2,474	2,751	2,445	5,936	85.2	24.5	109.7
15	XL Group plc	2,583	2,091	2,273	2,029	13,654	45.8	35.2	81.0
16	MAPFRE RE, Compania de Reaseguros S.A.[10]	2,289	2,071	1,724	1,508	1,283	62.8	25.2	87.9
17	R+V Versicherung AG[11]	2,164	2,120	2,136	2,092	2,349	73.5	24.6	98.0
18	The Toa Reinsurance Company, Limited[9,12]	2,067	1,857	2,067	1,857	1,501	72.8	24.7	97.5
19	Axis Capital Holdings Limited	2,021	1,915	2,021	1,915	5,867	54.1	31.9	86.0
20	RenaissanceRe Holdings Ltd.	2,011	1,416	2,011	1,416	4,732	32.0	32.7	64.7
21	MS Amlin plc[13]	1,930	1,588	1,930	1,588	2,741	47.1	31.1	78.2
22	Arch Capital Group Ltd.[14]	1,908	1,504	1,908	1,504	6,944	48.7	34.4	83.1
23	Assicurazioni Generali SpA	1,894	1,894	797	797	26,999	75.3	26.5	101.8
24	QBE Insurance Group Limited	1,624	1,023	1,624	1,023	10,560	45.9	37.5	83.4
25	Tokio Marine Holdings, Inc.[12,15]	1,546	1,339	1,546	1,339	29,152	54.5	38.4	92.9

1 All non-USD currencies converted to USD using foreign exchange rate at company's fiscal year-end.
2 As reported on Balance Sheet.
3 Nonlife only.
4 Net premium written data not reported; net premium earned substituted.
5 Lloyd's premiums are reinsurance only. Premiums for certain groups within the rankings also may include Lloyd's Syndicate premiums when applicable.
6 Total shareholders' funds includes Lloyd's members' assets and Lloyd's central reserves.
7 Loss and expense ratio detail not available on a GAAP basis.
8 Based on Everest Re Group Ltd. consolidated financial statements and includes Mt. Logan segment.
9 Fiscal year-end March 31, 2016.
10 Premium data excludes intergroup reinsurance.
11 Ratios are as reported and calculated on a gross basis.
12 Net asset value used for total shareholders' funds
13 MS Amlin data reflects legacy Amlin plc year-end 2015 results.
14 Based on Arch Capital Group Ltd. consolidated financial statements and includes Watford Re segment.
15 TSF of Tokio Marine Holdings Inc. at year-end Mar. 31, 2016, premium data based on Tokio Millennium Re AG year-end Dec. 31, 2015.

(N/A) - Information not applicable or not available at time of publication.
Source: A.M. Best

risks are so unusual or so large that they aren't covered in the insurance company's standard reinsurance treaties.

Reinsurers also can purchase reinsurance to cover their own risk exposure or to increase their capacity. This process is called a retrocession.

Developing Issues in Reinsurance

A.M. Best's 2016 *Review & Preview* report on the global reinsurance industry identifies several issues shaping the reinsurance industry, including the impact of merger activity and reinsurers' growing appetite for acquiring distributors such as managing general agents.

Over the past few years, reinsurers have made a number of strategic moves to position their organizations for long-term survival. Merger and acquisition activity is by far the most significant of these, with each deal having its own specific stated objective for a given organization.

Notable Classes of Reinsurance Companies

Class of 1992 (Hurricane Andrew)	Class of 2001 (9/11 Terror Attacks)	Class of 2005 (Katrina/Wilma/Rita)
Cat Ltd	Allied World	Ariel Re
Global Capital Re	Arch Capital	Flagstone
IPC Re	Aspen	Harbor Point
La Salle Re	AXIS	New Castle Re
Mid Ocean	Endurance	Lancashire
Partner Re	Max Re Capital	Validus
RenRe	Montpelier Re	
Tempest Reinsurance	Platinum Underwriters	
	DaVinci Re*	
	Olympus Re**	

Source: Company reports, BMA, A.M. Best data & research
*Sidecar by RenRe
**Sidecar by White Mountain Insurance Group
▨ Companies that have been acquired

Most transactions can be characterized as attempts to build scale, product and distribution capability, while improving operating and capital efficiency. It is not yet clear if all these objectives have been fully realized for the recently merged organizations. What is evident is that the acquired entities, which by and large were focused on U.S. property catastrophe reinsurance, are better off as part of a larger, more broadly diversified organization. While these transactions have done little to alleviate the excess capacity that exists in the market, they have provided the respective organizations far greater flexibility in deploying capacity across a broader spectrum of global opportunities. The broader product and distribution capability should also be a significant advantage in attracting capital market capacity as money managers seek to expand their horizons beyond property catastrophe risk.

In this regard, reinsurers increasingly seem to be viewing capital market capacity as an opportunity as opposed to a threat. Reinsurers are increasingly utilizing retrocessional capacity in various forms as a cycle management tool. Over the past few years, new sidecar facilities have been created or existing ones increased. Despite a progressive deterioration in pricing, terms and conditions, capital market capacity has continued to be attracted to the reinsurance sector, and underwriters that have the market knowledge and distribution capability to assess risk are benefiting. The capability to transfer risk to capital market facilities in exchange for fees and profit-sharing is a desirable alternative to have available for clients when risk-adjusted pricing prohibits the use of traditional balance sheet capacity. This is a trend that is expected to continue and expand beyond property classes. The formation of alternative asset vehicles such as Watford Re, ABR Re and Harrington Re are examples of where investors have become comfortable with a longer-term commitment of capital in exchange for narrower (re)insurance margins, enhanced with potential for stronger investment returns. There also seems to be a heightened awareness on the part of reinsurers, brokers and capital market participants alike, as to the value in getting closer to the risk/client. Reinsurers are well ahead on this front, generally through their insurance silos, which operate separately and distinctly from reinsurance operations.

More recently, providing capacity to MGA and MGU facilities is on the rise as capacity providers look for stable sources of business. There have been a number of strategic acquisitions or investments in MGAs by reinsurance companies and capital market facilities seeking to strengthen their distribution channel as traditional access to business continues to contract. Direct ownership of a distribution source serves the dual purpose of stabilizing the flow of business and reducing acquisition costs, while providing the insured client with a competitively priced product. Owning the MGA as opposed to just providing the capacity has the added benefit of greater ability in maintaining quality underwriting standards. History is littered with examples of losses resulting when the underwriting pen is given to an MGA without adequate alignment of interests.

The Growth of Alternative Capital

Alternative sources of capacity began to enter the market attracted by the increased reliability of risk models, diversification benefits and potential returns to investors. The low-yield environment that has been in place since the 2008 financial crisis has made these types of investments all the more compelling for investors.

The proliferation of efficient structures (sidecars) and insurance-linked securities (ILS) allowed for a shorter time horizon (one to three years), in addition to a relatively quick entry into and exit from the reinsurance market. Originally, reinsurers such as Hannover Re, Swiss Re and Munich Re were the leaders in the utilization of alternative capacity, largely provided by pension plans, sovereign wealth funds and hedge funds. The majority of this capacity was and has been deployed in the form of ILS and collateralized pools or temporary sidecars.

More recently, investors and users of this capacity are bypassing the traditional reinsurer and transferring risk directly to the capital markets. Lower interest rates have led to an increased inflow of alternative capital as investors look for uncorrelated ways to improve returns. This phenomenon has given rise to collateralized funds, unrated sidecars, more flexible forms of ILS and the birth of "Hedge Fund Re," looking to optimize investment returns offshore while building a base of long-term assets under management.

According to Guy Carpenter and A.M. Best data and research, today's convergence capacity totals $71 billion, supplementing the $340 billion available via traditional capacity in the global reinsurance market in the first half of 2016. Competition for U.S. property catastrophe business has been fierce since third-party capital exploded into the market (starting in earnest around 2006). The pressure has since rippled to other classes and geographies as capacity is reallocated.

Alternative Risk Transfer and Risk Financing

The blurring of boundaries between insurance and capital markets is most evident in structured finance, part of an area that is broadly known as alternative risk transfer (ART).

The highest-profile members of the ART community are captives—insurance or reinsurance companies owned by their insured clients and located in jurisdictions, or domiciles, that may be tax friendly or may have reduced capital and reserve requirements. Captives typically are formed by one or more noninsurance companies when traditional market coverage is more limited, or when the parent companies wish to have more direct control of their own risks.

Structured finance is a complex process of transferring risk, often with the purpose of raising capital. Much of the activity revolves around risk securitization, whereby the involved assets are not used as collateral as is typically found in a loan scenario. Instead, funds from investors are advanced to the originator based on the history of those assets, indicating a cash flow into the originator's business. The assets are then transferred by the originator to a separate legal entity—a special purpose vehicle (SPV)—that in turn issues securities to the investors. Interest and principal paid on those securities are financed by the cash flow.

Insurance-Linked Securities and Structured Transactions

Capital markets participants, reinsurers, brokers and insurers continue to collaborate in various combinations to create new risk-based offerings, including:

Natural Catastrophe Bonds: An alternative to reinsurance, these securities are used by insurers to protect themselves from natural catastrophes. Typically, they pay higher yields because investors could lose their entire stake in the event of a disaster. If the catastrophe happens, the funds go to the insurer to cover claims.

Global Reinsurance — Catastrophe Bond Transaction and Possible Outcomes

Transaction

Sponsor (Re)Insurer → **Premium** → Special Purpose Vehicle (SPV)

Principal → Special Purpose Vehicle (SPV) ← Capital Markets Investors

Special Purpose Vehicle (SPV) → **Coupon** → Capital Markets Investors

Return on capital trust claims payment ↑ Collateral Trust Account

Special Purpose Vehicle (SPV) ↓ **Principal (Proceeds)** → Collateral Trust Account

Possible Outcomes

Sponsor (Re)Insurer ← *If cat losses occur before maturity* ← Special Purpose Vehicle (SPV)

Special Purpose Vehicle (SPV) → **Principal** → Capital Markets Investors
If no cats occur before maturity

Principal to insurer to pay claims (insurance coverage) collateral agreement. ← Collateral Trust Account

Sources: International Monetary Fund, Artemis, A.M. Best research

Sidecars: Separate, limited purpose companies, generally formed and funded by investors (usually hedge funds) that work in tandem with insurance companies. The reinsurance sidecar purchases certain insurance policies from an insurer and shares in the profits and risks. It is a way for an insurer to share risk. If the policies have low claim rates while in possession of the sidecar, the investors will make higher returns.

Surplus Notes and Insurance Trust-Preferred CDOs: Surplus notes and trust-preferred CDOs (collateralized debt obligations) provide another funding source for small and midsize insurance companies that find it costly to issue capital on their own. These companies can access the capital markets through the use of the surplus notes/insurance trust-preferred pools. Securities in these pools are issued by a stand-alone SPV and sold to investors. The proceeds of the notes are used to purchase the transaction's collateral, which consists of surplus notes and insurance trust-preferred securities.

Embedded Value (Closed Block) Securitizations: An insurer can close a block of policies to new business and receive immediate cash from investors in exchange for some or all of the future earnings on that block of business. The pledged assets remain with the insurer and are potentially available in the event of an insolvency.

Catastrophe Bond Issuance – P/C-Related Risks
(US$ millions)

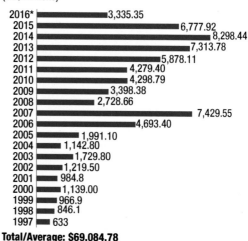

2016*	3,335.35
2015	6,777.92
2014	8,298.44
2013	7,313.78
2012	5,878.11
2011	4,279.40
2010	4,298.79
2009	3,398.38
2008	2,728.66
2007	7,429.55
2006	4,693.40
2005	1,991.10
2004	1,142.80
2003	1,729.80
2002	1,219.50
2001	984.8
2000	1,139.00
1999	966.9
1998	846.1
1997	633

Total/Average: $69,084.78

Source: A.M. Best data & research
*Through June 30, 2016

Securitization of Structured Settlements: A structured settlement is an annuity used for settling personal injury, product liability, medical malpractice and wrongful death cases. The defendant (typically, a liability insurer) discharges its obligation by purchasing an annuity from a highly rated life insurance company. Securitization of annuity cash flows is achieved through the use of a bankruptcy-remote SPV. The issuer of the securities, the SPV, raises funds from investors that are used to purchase annuity cash flows from the annuitants. The cash flows received by the issuer are used primarily to service the principal and interest payments due the investors.

Mortality Catastrophe Bonds: Investors in these bonds lose money only if a level of deaths linked to a catastrophic event exceeds a certain threshold. The event's trigger is extreme (for example, a pandemic). These are a derivative of natural cat bonds.

Life Settlement Securitizations: A life settlement contract is a way for a policyholder to liquidate a life insurance policy. A portfolio of these contracts may be securitized to provide a source of capital. However, certain variables, such as regulatory issues and the uncertainties associated with predicting life expectancies, can create obstacles that may slow their path to the marketplace.

Securitization of Reinsurance Recoverables: Insurance and reinsurance companies have been finding alternative ways to reduce their exposure to uncollectible recoverables and reduce the concentration risk associated with ceded exposures. One approach is the securitization of reinsurance recoverables, which involves a structured debt instrument that transfers risk associated with the risk of uncollectible reinsurance to the capital markets. This risk transfer may also be accomplished through the use of collateralized debt obligation (CDO) technology.

Spotlight: The New Risks of Energy

Discussions of emerging risks often start with cyber exposure and new threats of epidemics, but energy, whether it's petrochemical or solar based, continues to present new risk exposures.

The steady decline of oil prices means healthy margins for petrochemical facilities selling directly to consumers and for storage and transportation sectors, but lower costs create problems in other areas. "This has a twofold impact," said Tim Kania, global head of energy and construction for Aspen Insurance, identifying upstream— exploration and production—and downstream, or petrochemical.

"On the upstream energy side, with the price of commodity decreasing steadily ... we've seen reduced drilling occurring in a lot of the assets around the world, a reduced amount of new construction projects starting because of the reduced need for drilling, and also some of the exposure base being reduced and drilling activities subsiding as it becomes less economically viable to conduct the drilling based on the revenue expected from the lower commodity prices," Kania said.

"This has an impact on the insurance perspective as well, with reduced values, reduced business interruption values in the upstream energy market, and it also has some concern with the financial well-being of some of these clients," he added.

"As financial constraints come into play because of lower revenue levels or reduced availabilities, it may put pressure on the industry to reduce required maintenance, which could lead to claims in the future, but to date, we haven't seen a dramatic impact on that effect yet," Kania said. "That will take a period of time for it to manifest itself, and it's an important consideration when underwriting these exposures, to consider the prior levels of maintenance and capex that were deployed and to make sure that that continues in the future."

Midstream operations and contractors also have been affected, according to John O'Brien, president of the environmental product line at Ironshore.

"We've seen companies whose sales have gone from $300 million to $80 million in the course of two years," O'Brien said, adding it's not all bad news. "We write some downstream refiners, which actually, the refiners have done very well in the market."

Energy-related risks, however, reach beyond fossil fuels.

"There are a lot of exposures when it comes to dealing with photovoltaics that people don't really take into consideration," said Skip Donnell, technical director of the engineering technical unit of Liberty Mutual.

"A lot of these installations, particularly the commercial installations, are ... on flat roof decks," explained James Breitkreitz, executive technical director for risk engineering, Zurich NA. "You're now introducing a fairly significant electrical system into an area where typically there isn't much of an exposure. We have ignition sources that we never had to think about. In addition to that, we're adding combustible loading to the roof. We're also changing the way that the roof deck will burn and react to a fire."

A fire on a solar-paneled roof leads to additional risks.

"When you start putting photovoltaics up on the roof of a building, the dynamic of how a firefighter fights a fire changes dramatically," Donnell said. "As a result, you may see situations where they don't go on top of the roof like they used to, to fight a fire."

The best way to mitigate solar power-related issues? "Work closely with your broker and your insurance company," Donnell said. "Find a group that works well with you. Put together a plan of action that will identify the problems and help you put together a long-term solution that will allow you to move toward this new energy source but

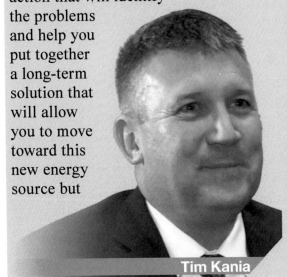

Tim Kania

make sure your facility is as safe as possible."

"We certainly don't want to discourage anybody from installing solar panels, wonderful technology," Zurich's Breitkreitz said. "But they have to do it right. That's what Zurich Risk Engineering does. We help our customers control these risks and install these things the right way."

Despite the new risks around energy, Ironshore's O'Brien sees blue skies ahead.

"We're continuing to innovate and provide relevant policies that speak to the needs of customers," he said. "There's a lot of capacity. People talk about it, but if you're relevant, you can always make a difference in insurance. We're pretty bullish on it."

There are other positive changes as well, Kania noted.

"Environmentally friendly exposures and assets continue to be a growing trend in the U.S. and around the world," Kania said. "This flight to going green seems to be very popular. Coupled with lower commodity pricing, it has allowed a lot of the utility industry to retire some of their less efficient fossil-fueled power plants and replace them with higher efficiency natural gas combined-cycle power plants. They also capitalize on a lower cost for the fuel source of natural gas, which allows additional investment and spending in that area."

Insurance Stands the Traditional Business Cycle on Its Head

Most industries work as follows:

- Build product.
- Incur costs.
- Price product.
- Sell product.
- Generate revenue.

But insurance works largely in reverse:

- Build product.
- Price product.
- Sell product.
- Generate revenue.
- Incur costs.

The significance of this reversed revenue/cost cycle is that the product is priced and sold based on an estimate of future costs to be incurred. These estimates can be wrong for any number of reasons, including catastrophes, claim cost inflation, changes in legal climate, newly identified exposures not known at the time the insurance policy was sold, social changes, investment market fluctuations and other factors.

This means that insurers must be very good at predicting the future and very prudent in administering their business over the long term. It directly results in what are known as underwriting cycles. It's also an important reason why the number of insurance insolvencies sometimes spikes in periods following catastrophes or market disruptions.

The insurance industry is less tangible in that the actual cost of its product isn't precisely known at the time of sale. The true cost is determined at a later point, often much later. Yet risk is taken on along with unpredictable, exogenous factors that ultimately determine profit or loss. While insurers gauge the probability of a large catastrophic event or some latent liability, these scenarios still cause a supply shock. A simplified explanation is that the insurance cycle is driven by supply and demand. If capacity is lacking, the price of risk goes up. Too much capacity and prices drift down. At some point, the downward drift is too far and balance sheets end up in need of repair, A.M. Best's annual report on the global reinsurance industry noted.

Fiscal Fitness

When insurance companies in the United States fall on tough times, they cannot file for bankruptcy, because the U.S. Bankruptcy Code excludes them. Instead, state law applies to insurance companies in poor financial shape.

Insurance companies are monitored and regulated by state insurance departments that seek to protect policyholders from the risk of a company in financial distress. When a company is unable to meet its obligations, the insurance commissioner in the company's home state initiates a process to help the company regain its financial footing. This period is known as rehabilitation.

By obtaining control of a company, the insurance department becomes the rehabilitator or liquidator of the company. The commissioner also may retain a special deputy receiver to supervise the company's activities. The receiver may be an employee of the state insurance department or an independent professional experienced in legal, accounting and actuarial issues.

The receiver oversees an accounting of the company's assets and liabilities and administers the estate of the company. If it is determined that the company cannot be rehabilitated, the company is declared insolvent, and the laws of the state require the commissioner to ask the state court to order liquidation.

As a condition of doing business in most states, all insurance companies are members of a guaranty fund or association—nonprofit organizations created to protect policyholders.

The members are assessed a percentage of applicable premiums, which is used to meet the claims of policyholders in that state should an insolvency occur. Each state typically has one or more guaranty associations, with each one dealing with certain types of insurance. By statute, guaranty funds contain upper limits to the amount they can pay, commonly $300,000.

Although guaranty funds generally provide a measure of recovery, consumers and taxpayers likely will take a hit from an insolvency. To recoup losses, insurers that helped to pay claims of an insolvent insurer may assess surcharges on customers' insurance bills. States, in turn, may reduce those insurers' tax burdens, resulting in less revenue for the state.

Impairment studies by A.M. Best that focused on the U.S. life/lealth industry have noted that the primary cause for historical impairments, in general, has been deficient loss reserves/inadequate pricing.

Most of the companies listed were younger than the industry average and median ages, although during the past decade a few venerable companies failed. The financially impaired companies were also generally smaller, in terms of net premiums and surplus, than the average for the life insurance industry overall.

Another report on impairments said of the property/casualty sector: "The financial health of the insurance industry is affected not only by general economic factors but also by catastrophes and underwriting issues that are not necessarily correlated directly with economic activity. ... Economic activity generally is related inversely to impairments—the lower the economic activity, the higher the number of impairments and vice versa."

Overview of Best's Credit Rating Evaluation

This section is from *Best's Credit Rating Methodology: Global Life and Non-Life Insurance Edition*. The primary objective of Best's Credit Ratings within the insurance segment is to provide an opinion of the rated entity's ability to meet its senior financial obligations, which for an operating insurance company are its ongoing insurance policy and contract obligations. The assignment of a Best's Credit Rating is derived from an in-depth evaluation of a company's balance sheet strength, operating performance and business profile, as compared with A.M. Best's quantitative and qualitative standards.

In determining a company's ability to meet its current and ongoing obligations, the most important area to evaluate is its balance sheet strength, since it is the foundation for financial security. Balance sheet strength measures the exposure of a company's equity or surplus to volatility based on its operating and financial practices, and can reflect its capital-generation capabilities resulting from quality of earnings. One of the primary tools used to evaluate an insurer's balance sheet strength is Best's Capital Adequacy Ratio (BCAR), which provides a quantitative measure of the risks inherent in a company's investment and insurance profile, relative to its risk-adjusted capital. A.M. Best's analysis of the balance sheet also encompasses a thorough review of various financial tests and ratios over five-year and in some cases 10-year periods.

The assessment of balance sheet strength includes an analysis of an organization's regulatory filings at the operating insurance company, holding company and consolidated levels. To assess the financial strength and financial flexibility of a rated entity, a variety of balance sheet, income statement and cash-flow metrics are reviewed, including corporate capital structure, financial leverage, interest expense coverage, cash coverage, liquidity, capital generation, and historical sources and uses of capital.

While balance sheet strength is the foundation for financial security, it provides an assessment of capital adequacy at a point in time. A.M. Best views operating performance and business profile as leading indicators when measuring future balance sheet strength and long-term financial stability.

The term "future" is the key, since ratings are prospective and go well beyond a "static" balance sheet view. Profitability is the engine that ultimately drives capital, and looking out into the future enables the analyst to gauge a company's ability to preserve and/or generate new capital over time. In many respects, what determines the relative strength or weakness of a company's operating performance is a combination of its business profile and its ability to effectively execute its strategy.

Rating Translation Table

FSR	Long-Term ICR	FSR	Long-Term ICR
A++	aaa	B	bb+
	aa+		bb
A+	aa	B-	bb-
	aa-	C++	b+
A	a+		b
	a	C+	b-
A-	a-	C	ccc+
B++	bbb+		ccc
	bbb	C-	ccc-
B+	bbb-		cc
		D	c

A company exhibiting strong performance over time will generate earnings sufficient to maintain a prudent level of risk-adjusted capital and optimize stakeholder value. Strong performers are those companies whose earnings are relatively consistent and deemed to be sustainable. Companies with a stable track record and better than average earnings power may receive higher ratings and have lower risk-adjusted capital relative to their peers.

On the other hand, companies that have demonstrated weaknesses in their earnings—through either consistent losses or volatility—are more likely to struggle to maintain or improve capital in the future. For these reasons, these companies typically are rated lower than their counterparts that perform well and usually are held to higher than minimum capital guidelines to minimize the chance of being downgraded if established trends were to continue.

A.M. Best believes that risk management is the common thread that links balance sheet strength, operating performance and business profile. Risk management fundamentals can be found in the strategic decision-making process used by a company to define its business profile, and in the various financial management practices and operating elements of an insurer that dictate the sustainability of its operating performance and, ultimately, its exposure to capital volatility. Therefore, if a company is practicing sound risk management and executing its strategy effectively, it will preserve and build its balance sheet strength and perform successfully over the long term—both key elements of A.M. Best's ratings and the evaluation of risk management.

A.M. Best's Insurance Information Products And Services

Insight and Advantage

A.M. Best provides dozens of insurance information resources that help everyone from C-level executives to independent agents work more effectively and productively. The resources provide unique insight—based on more than a century of exclusive focus on the insurance industry—that delivers a competitive advantage to those who need to know the why as well as the what, for tomorrow as well as today.

Below is a sampling of some of A.M. Best's most widely used and highly regarded products and services. For more product offerings, visit *www.ambest.com/sales*.

Best's Insurance Reports®: A.M. Best's flagship product provides in-depth *AMB Credit Reports* on thousands of insurers, reinsurers and groups around the world. The reports present a company's current Best's Credit Rating, a Rating Rationale that explains why the rating was assigned, commentary on the company's risk management strategy, an analysis of its balance sheet strength, and more. *Best's Insurance Reports* is available online via *BestLink®*, A.M. Best's sophisticated data delivery and integration platform.

BEST'S FINANCIAL STRENGTH RATING GUIDE – (FSR)

A Best's Financial Strength Rating (FSR) is an independent opinion of an insurer's financial strength and ability to meet its ongoing insurance policy and contract obligations. An FSR is not assigned to specific insurance policies or contracts and does not address any other risk, including, but not limited to, an insurer's claims-payment policies or procedures; the ability of the insurer to dispute or deny claims payment on grounds of misrepresentation or fraud; or any specific liability contractually borne by the policy or contract holder. An FSR is not a recommendation to purchase, hold or terminate any insurance policy, contract or any other financial obligation issued by an insurer, nor does it address the suitability of any particular policy or contract for a specific purpose or purchaser. In addition, an FSR may be displayed with a rating identifier, modifier or affiliation code that denotes a unique aspect of the opinion.

Best's Financial Strength Rating (FSR) Scale

Rating Categories	Rating Symbols	Rating Notches*	Category Definitions
Superior	A+	A++	Assigned to insurance companies that have, in our opinion, a superior ability to meet their ongoing insurance obligations.
Excellent	A	A-	Assigned to insurance companies that have, in our opinion, an excellent ability to meet their ongoing insurance obligations.
Good	B+	B++	Assigned to insurance companies that have, in our opinion, a good ability to meet their ongoing insurance obligations.
Fair	B	B-	Assigned to insurance companies that have, in our opinion, a fair ability to meet their ongoing insurance obligations. Financial strength is vulnerable to adverse changes in underwriting and economic conditions.
Marginal	C+	C++	Assigned to insurance companies that have, in our opinion, a marginal ability to meet their ongoing insurance obligations. Financial strength is vulnerable to adverse changes in underwriting and economic conditions.
Weak	C	C-	Assigned to insurance companies that have, in our opinion, a weak ability to meet their ongoing insurance obligations. Financial strength is very vulnerable to adverse changes in underwriting and economic conditions.
Poor	D	-	Assigned to insurance companies that have, in our opinion, a poor ability to meet their ongoing insurance obligations. Financial strength is extremely vulnerable to adverse changes in underwriting and economic conditions.

*Each Best's Financial Strength Rating Category from "A+" to "C" includes a Rating Notch to reflect a gradation of financial strength within the category. A Rating Notch is expressed with either a second plus "+" or a minus "-".

FSR Non-Rating Designations

Designation Symbols	Designation Definitions
E	Status assigned to insurance companies that are publicly placed under a significant form of regulatory supervision, control or restraint - including cease and desist orders, conservatorship or rehabilitation, but not liquidation - that prevents conduct of normal ongoing insurance operations; an impaired insurer.
F	Status assigned to insurance companies that are publicly placed in liquidation by a court of law or by a forced liquidation; an impaired insurer.
S	Status assigned to rated insurance companies to suspend the outstanding FSR when sudden and significant events impact operations and rating implications cannot be evaluated due to a lack of timely or adequate information; or in cases where continued maintenance of the previously published rating opinion is in violation of evolving regulatory requirements.
NR	Status assigned to insurance companies that are not rated; may include previously rated insurance companies or insurance companies that have never been rated by AMBRS.

Rating Disclosure: Use and Limitations

A Best's Credit Rating (BCR) is a forward-looking independent and objective opinion regarding an insurer's, issuer's or financial obligation's relative creditworthiness. The opinion represents a comprehensive analysis consisting of a quantitative and qualitative evaluation of balance sheet strength, operating performance and business profile or, where appropriate, the specific nature and details of a security. Because a BCR is a forward-looking opinion as of the date it is released, it cannot be considered as a fact or guarantee of future credit quality and therefore cannot be described as accurate or inaccurate. A BCR is a relative measure of risk that implies credit quality and is assigned using a scale with a defined population of categories and notches. Entities or obligations assigned the same BCR symbol developed using the same scale, should not be viewed as completely identical in terms of credit quality. Alternatively, they are alike in category (or notches within a category), but given there is a prescribed progression of categories (and notches) used in assigning the ratings of a much larger population of entities or obligations, the categories (notches) cannot mirror the precise subtleties of risk that are inherent within similarly rated entities or obligations. While a BCR reflects the opinion of A.M. Best Rating Services, Inc. (AMBRS) of relative creditworthiness, it is not an indicator or predictor of defined impairment or default probability with respect to any specific insurer, issuer or financial obligation. A BCR is not investment advice, nor should it be construed as a consulting or advisory service, as such; it is not intended to be utilized as a recommendation to purchase, hold or terminate any insurance policy, contract, security or any other financial obligation, nor does it address the suitability of any particular policy or contract for a specific purpose or purchaser. Users of a BCR should not rely on it in making any investment decision; however, if used, the BCR must be considered as only one factor. Users must make their own evaluation of each investment decision. A BCR opinion is provided on an "as is" basis without any expressed or implied warranty. In addition, a BCR may be changed, suspended or withdrawn at any time for any reason at the sole discretion of AMBRS.

BCRs are distributed via the AMBRS website at *www.ambest.com*. For additional information regarding the development of a BCR and other rating-related information and definitions, including outlooks, modifiers, identifiers and affiliation codes, please refer to the report titled "Understanding Best's Credit Ratings" available at no charge on the AMBRS website. BCRs are proprietary and may not be reproduced without permission.
Copyright © 2016 A.M. Best Company, Inc. and/or its affiliates. ALL RIGHTS RESERVED. **Version 090116**

A.M. Best's Financial Suite: This family of databases presents detailed information from the financial statements of thousands of insurance entities. *Financial Suite* products are all accessible online via *BestLink*. Custom presentations of data are also available.

- *Best's Statement File – US* presents complete statement data for U.S. insurers;

BEST'S ISSUER CREDIT RATING GUIDE - (ICR)

A Best's Issuer Credit Rating (ICR) is an independent opinion of an entity's ability to meet its ongoing financial obligations and can be issued on either a long- or short-term basis. A long-term ICR is an opinion of an entity's ability to meet its ongoing senior financial obligations, while a short-term ICR is an opinion of an entity's ability to meet its ongoing financial obligations with original maturities generally less than one year. An ICR is an opinion regarding the relative future credit risk of an entity. Credit risk is the risk that an entity may not meet its contractual financial obligations as they come due. An ICR does not address any other risk. In addition, an ICR is not a recommendation to buy, sell or hold any securities, contracts or any other financial obligations, nor does it address the suitability of any particular financial obligation for a specific purpose or purchaser. An ICR may be displayed with a rating identifier or modifier that denotes a unique aspect of the opinion.

Best's Long-Term Issuer Credit Rating (ICR) Scale

Rating Categories	Rating Symbols	Rating Notches*	Category Definitions
Exceptional	aaa	-	Assigned to entities that have, in our opinion, an exceptional ability to meet their ongoing senior financial obligations.
Superior	aa	aa+ / aa-	Assigned to entities that have, in our opinion, a superior ability to meet their ongoing senior financial obligations.
Excellent	a	a+ / a-	Assigned to entities that have, in our opinion, an excellent ability to meet their ongoing senior financial obligations.
Good	bbb	bbb+ / bbb-	Assigned to entities that have, in our opinion, a good ability to meet their ongoing senior financial obligations.
Fair	bb	bb+ / bb-	Assigned to entities that have, in our opinion, a fair ability to meet their ongoing senior financial obligations. Credit quality is vulnerable to adverse changes in industry and economic conditions.
Marginal	b	b+ / b-	Assigned to entities that have, in our opinion, a marginal ability to meet their ongoing senior financial obligations. Credit quality is vulnerable to adverse changes in industry and economic conditions
Weak	ccc	ccc+ / ccc-	Assigned to entities that have, in our opinion, a weak ability to meet their ongoing senior financial obligations. Credit quality is vulnerable to adverse changes in industry and economic conditions.
Very Weak	cc	-	Assigned to entities that have, in our opinion, a very weak ability to meet their ongoing senior financial obligations. Credit quality is very vulnerable to adverse changes in industry and economic conditions.
Poor	c	-	Assigned to entities that have, in our opinion, a poor ability to meet their ongoing senior financial obligations. Credit quality is extremely vulnerable to adverse changes in industry and economic conditions.

Best's Long-Term Issuer Credit Rating Categories from "aa" to "ccc" include Rating Notches to reflect a gradation within the category to indicate whether credit quality is near the top or bottom of a particular Rating Category. Rating Notches are expressed with a "+" (plus) or "-" (minus).

Best's Short-Term Issuer Credit Rating (ICR) Scale

Rating Categories	Rating Symbols	Category Definitions
Strongest	AMB-1+	Assigned to entities that have, in our opinion, the strongest ability to repay their short-term financial obligations.
Outstanding	AMB-1	Assigned to entities that have, in our opinion, an outstanding ability to repay their short-term financial obligations.
Satisfactory	AMB-2	Assigned to entities that have, in our opinion, a satisfactory ability to repay their short-term financial obligations.
Adequate	AMB-3	Assigned to entities that have, in our opinion, an adequate ability to repay their short-term financial obligations; however, adverse industry or economic conditions likely will reduce their capacity to meet their financial commitments.
Questionable	AMB-4	Assigned to entities that have, in our opinion, questionable credit quality and are vulnerable to adverse economic or other external changes, which could have a marked impact on their ability to meet their financial commitments.

Long- and Short-Term ICR Non-Rating Designations

Designation Symbols	Designation Definitions
d	Status assigned to entities (excluding insurers) that are in default or when a bankruptcy petition or similar action has been filed and made public.
e	Status assigned to insurers that are publicly placed under a significant form of regulatory supervision, control or restraint - including cease and desist orders, conservatorship or rehabilitation, but not liquidation - that prevents conduct of normal ongoing operations; an impaired entity.
f	Status assigned to insurers that are publicly placed in liquidation by a court of law or by a forced liquidation; an impaired entity.
s	Status assigned to rated entities to suspend the outstanding ICR when sudden and significant events impact operations and rating implications cannot be evaluated due to a lack of timely or adequate information; or in cases where continued maintenance of the previously published rating opinion is in violation of evolving regulatory requirements.
nr	Status assigned to entities that are not rated; may include previously rated entities or entities that have never been rated by AMBRS.

Rating Disclosure: Use and Limitations

A Best's Credit Rating (BCR) is a forward-looking independent and objective opinion regarding an insurer's, issuer's or financial obligation's relative creditworthiness. The opinion represents a comprehensive analysis consisting of a quantitative and qualitative evaluation of balance sheet strength, operating performance and business profile or, where appropriate, the specific nature and details of a security. Because a BCR is a forward-looking opinion as of the date it is released, it cannot be considered as a fact or guarantee of future credit quality and therefore cannot be described as accurate or inaccurate. A BCR is a relative measure of risk that implies credit quality and is assigned using a scale with a defined population of categories and notches. Entities or obligations assigned the same BCR symbol developed using the same scale, should not be viewed as completely identical in terms ofcredit quality. Alternatively, they are alike in category (or notches within a category), but given there is a prescribed progression of categories (and notches) used in assigning the ratings of a much larger population of entities or obligations, the categories (notches) cannot mirror the precise subtleties of risk that are inherent within similarly rated entities or obligations. While a BCR reflects the opinion of A.M. Best Rating Services Inc. (AMBRS) of relative creditworthiness, it is not an indicator or predictor of defined impairment or default probability with respect to any specific insurer, issuer or financial obligation. A BCR is not investment advice, nor should it be construed as a consulting or advisory service, as such; it is not intended to be utilized as a recommendation to purchase, hold or terminate any insurance policy, contract, security or any other financial obligation, nor does it address the suitability of any particular policy or contract for a specific purpose or purchaser. Users of a BCR should not rely on it in making any investment decision; however, if used, the BCR must be considered as only one factor. Users must make their own evaluation of each investment decision. A BCR opinion is provided on an "as is" basis without any expressed or implied warranty. In addition, a BCR may be changed, suspended or withdrawn at any time for any reason at the sole discretion of AMBRS.

BCRs are distributed via the AMBRS website at *www.ambest.com*. For additional information regarding the development of a BCR and other rating-related information and definitions, including outlooks, modifiers, identifiers and affiliation codes, please refer to the report titled "Understanding Best's Credit Ratings" available at no charge on the AMBRS website. BCRs are proprietary and may not be reproduced without permission.
Version 090116

additional databases focus on market share, loss reserves, expenses and investments.

- Financial information on more than 16,000 non-U.S. insurers worldwide is presented in *Best's Statement File – Global.*
- *Best's Statement File – Canada* offers regulatory data from filings made with the Office of the Superintendent of Financial Institutions (OSFI) for hundreds of Canadian property/casualty or life/health insurers. Other region-specific editions of *Best's Statement File* cover the United Kingdom and Latin America, as well as Asia-Pacific and the Middle East/North Africa regions.

Best's Capital Adequacy Ratio Adjustment System – Property/Casualty, US: This desktop application provides insight into how changing conditions can affect a company's future claims-paying ability with the same base model A.M. Best analysts use to calculate the Best's Capital Adequacy Ratio (BCAR) score for single and group U.S. property/casualty companies. A.M. Best also offers ***Best's Capital Adequacy Ratio Model – Universal*** for the non-U.S. life and nonlife sectors.

Best's Aggregates & Averages – US & Canada (Property/Casualty and Life/Health editions): This vital benchmarking and strategic-planning tool presents current and historical consolidated data for the property/casualty or life/health industry.

Best's Key Rating Guide – US & Canada (Property/Casualty and Life/Health editions): This classic resource offers, online and in print, five years of key financial figures and Best's Credit Ratings for thousands of insurance companies and HMOs—plus personalized reports that display information on individual companies in a format ideal for client presentations and proposals.

Best's Underwriting Guide and ***Best's Loss Control Manual***: These online risk management resources provide detailed reports on hundreds of businesses, industries and municipal services, written from either the underwriter's or loss control engineer's point of view.

Best's Agent Center™: This convenient, cost-effective online center brings together a variety of A.M. Best resources that are useful for the community-focused, independent agent.

Best's Insurance News & Analysis: This subscription-based service provides the full scope of A.M. Best's award-winning news and industry research, all accessible through a streamlined web portal. The following are some products the service includes:

- *Best's Journal*, a compilation of ratings-related research and analysis.
- *BestWeek®*, a recap of the top stories for the global insurance industry.
- *Best's Special Reports* and *Best's Statistical Studies*, in-depth coverage of critical topics from an analytical or data-driven approach.

- *Best's Regulatory Week*, a review of insurance-related regulatory and legislative actions.
- *Best's Review®*, A.M. Best's award-winning monthly insurance magazine.
- *BestDay®*, a digest of insurance news from the past 24 hours.

A.M. Best also publishes a variety of online reports on individual companies, by state/by line market segments, peer group composites and other selections of information to meet your research and analysis needs. Visit *www.ambest.com/sales* for a complete overview of all that A.M. Best has to offer, or call (800) 424-2378 or (908) 439-2200, ext. 5742.

39440681R00038

Made in the USA
Middletown, DE
15 January 2017